FORTUNE'S IMPASSE

Saving the Family's Jewels

TIM MALONEY
RANDY MCLACHLAN

Copyright © 2013 by Tim Maloney and Randy McLachlan
All rights reserved.

This book or any portion thereof may not be reproduced or used in any manner whatsoever without the express written permission of the authors except for the use of brief quotations in a book review.

Printed in the United States of America
First Printing, 2013

ISBN-10: 1484076524
ISBN-13: 978-1484076521

For information address: Newport Press
3096 Balmoral Ave., Burlington, Ontario L7N 1E4
www.fortunesimpasse.com

Dedicated to Business Families Everywhere

The family is one of nature's masterpieces.
~George Santayana, *The Life of Reason*

Foreword

Toward the end of the 1920s in Europe, having experienced many of life's most heart-rending trials, my grandpa, Andy, summoned the courage to immigrate in search of a new life for his young wife, Lena, and his ailing two-year-old son, Joe—my father. Andy became a successful entrepreneur, and he raised a wonderful family, now thriving in its fifth generation. I have long been inspired by Andy's courage and dedication to future generations, and I have inherited his passion for our family business.

There is nothing more compelling in life than trying to understand the dynamics of family relationships, both in the families we are born into and the families we create. As parents, we are often overwhelmed by the challenges of providing love, nurturing and financial security to our children. These needs change rapidly through the cycles of a family's life. Fortunately, fact-based study and analysis of successful families over the last few decades now shines a light on the ways and best practices that can help us learn and grow—as individuals and as a family.

Most of our fulfillment in life comes from the success of our relationships within our families. My grandpa referred to these as the simple things in life that bring us the greatest joy. Truth be told, there is nothing simple about managing a family's human, intellectual and financial capital from generation to generation.

The message inside *Fortune's Impasse* is for all those who have sought or still seek the courage and inspiration to make their family life—and all relationships in the family—the very best they can be, for generations to come.

John E. Peller
President & CEO
Andrew Peller Limited
www.andrewpeller.com

Preface

Dan Fortune gave up his personal dreams and aspirations on the sudden death of his father to salvage a rundown community food market, and to provide for his mother. Through hard work, skill and good luck, Dan grew that local market into a major chain of markets and a vertically integrated food business.

Despite this apparent success, Dan felt that things were out of control. Life was complex, too complex. His wife Marnie felt that their family was falling apart and internal strife between his two eldest children, who were both vying to run the business, threatened to undo everything that he and Marnie had worked so hard to build.

Out of desperation, Dan and Marnie reached out to their trusted friend and business partner Ben Curtis. Ben had already successfully transitioned his family real estate development business to the next generation. Ben referred Dan and Marnie to the folks who had guided him and his wife Ginny and their family successfully through their own transition.

Dan and Marnie embarked on their own succession journey. Guided by the GBA team, they apply a unique succession management system.

Dan eventually gains clarity and control over his situation, learning what options are both possible and most appropriate in their circumstances.

For those who are involved in a family business or a business family in any capacity, Fortune's Impasse will provide *inspiration, hope* and *guidance* on how to achieve clarity, control and a good outcome for everyone involved.

Acknowledgements

Tim Maloney

Family businesses have been and will continue to be the economic backbone of many countries throughout the world. Supporting and being of assistance to various businesses like these from start-up to more mature stages of their growth has been a privilege.

I would like to acknowledge my co-author Randy McLachlan and his firm Genbridge Family Offices Inc. I don't believe either of us initially made our contribution of thought to the areas in which we work with the idea that we had to write a book. Rather it was the subject matter that took hold of us. Fortune's Impasse was written so that people, families could read it and know that they weren't alone in struggling with common problems in succession and transition.

As someone who felt comfortable dealing with operating companies, I recognized and appreciated Randy's insights into the areas that impact the "business family." He understands their interaction with the business itself, including the interpersonal dynamics and the legal, financial and taxation requirements. The rigor with which he and his office pursue excellence is impressive, and I have come to know that his empathy for the human element of the business family is never far from his thoughts.

We all do what we do mostly through what others leave in us day to day. I owe a great deal to my father and mother for what they have shaped in me and what both continue to shape in me in the winter of their own lives. Through my sister, brothers and in-laws, I have been blessed with a large and multi-talented extended family, and a wonderful group of lifelong friends.

Finally to my wife Lori and our children Zac, Brooke and Gillian, what we have created so far has been a life full of opportunities. We all have been able to experience the challenges and victories that full lives bring. The ride continues.

Randy W. McLachlan

I would like to start with acknowledging my co-author, Tim Maloney. Tim, through his persistent efforts to understand what I really did, managed to "tease out" a more clear articulation of our process than we had ever done on our own. We discovered that we followed very similar processes: his applied to the businesses that he worked with and ours applied to the families that we worked with. Tim then strong encouraged us to write a book to get our message out. When he saw the more technical approach that we initially took to this book, he intervened and took the initiative to give it a more reader friendly face.

I wish to acknowledge our clients. Many dozens of families have entrusted us to provide service and guidance to them and their businesses for over twenty years. Through their sharing of dreams, visions, goals, passions, fears and concerns, we have been given the rare privilege to apply our various technical skills to help them navigate the rugged shores of family succession. Along the way many have encouraged us to write about what we do and how we do it, but not about them. We hope that we have found the right balance in this regard, for our clients' privacy is paramount.

My family, parents and siblings, have provided the greatest motivation for both what I do day to day and for this book. I am amongst the third generation of a family farm business that is currently transitioning into its 5th generation. My experience as a child, youth and young adult, made me never want to be part of a "family business". After years spent in the pursuit and application of technical knowledge in the fields of law, accounting, finance, business and serving families and their businesses, I realized that my greatest insights and lessons have come from my formative years growing up in a family business on the farm.

Table of Contents

Part I 1
    The Cottage 3
    Not so Fast 11
    Pulling the Plug 15
    Dan at the Helm 21
    Another Shoe Drops 27
    Ben's Big Idea 35
    Hold, Fold or Double Down 43

Part II 53
    Salad Days 55
    The Next-Generation Women 61
    The Bust 69
    Big Brother 75
    Big Trouble 81
    The Boss 87
    Avoidance 97
    The Fortune Huddle 103

Part III 109
    Ben's Island 111
    Fore! 117
    A New Arrival 123
    The Family Office 133
    Losing Sleep 139
    Just Between Us 149
    $F^{3®}$—What Does "Good" Look Like? 157
    The Founders 167

What is Money for? 179
Gaining Other Perspectives 187
The Next Generation: Who, How and Why 193
The Lunch 203
The Firm 211
Strategic Thinking 219
Fanny and Jeff 227
Inge and Jimmy Explain 243
The Family Weighs In 251
Finding Clarity 265
Copper Beech 269
Postscript 277

Part I

The Cottage

Dan Fortune sat on his cottage deck admiring the sun setting over the waters of the bay on which his summer home was situated. A seaplane floated in its mooring next to his dock, bobbing gently. It sure beat trying to deal with the traffic, he told himself.

He had been out walking around the cottage property, stopping to give the tire swing on the big old copper beech tree a push, remembering the days when it had been his children's favorite place to play. The tree was 150 feet high and the previous owner had told him, at that time, that it was a century tree and might live to be 300 years old. Now it was well past its sesquicentennial—kind of midlife, Dan decided.

The cottage had been one of his early rewards to himself, and the copper a prime factor in why he'd wanted the spot in the first place. The big tree spoke to him as a symbol of strength, resiliency and shared values—three attributes he thought were positive aspirations. He moved out from its shade and headed back inside.

If only my life was as tranquil, he mused. My whole existence is so darn complex these days. I'm not having near the fun I thought I'd be able to have, that I should be able to have. My lifestyle should be improving, yet I feel like every time I get free something sucks me backwards into matters that need my attention. I could get clear of things if there were only three or four of me.

In his early 70s, he still had his health, if not the vitality he once felt in every aspect of his life. Sure there had been that scare with his prostate six or seven years back, but the medical team had given him a relatively clean bill of health after his treatments.

Whenever his friends or employees asked about his health, he would reply, "They should be knocking off copies of me somewhere." He didn't fail to follow up with a comment or two on what they should be doing to monitor their own well-being.

"If it could happen to me, it could happen to anybody," he always finished.

One of Dan's most endearing qualities was his sense of loyalty to those he had known throughout his life. He gave it and expected it in return.

He was a networker before someone, somewhere, had decided there should be a term for being civil and helping others out when you could. He had decided early that if mutual benefit was an outcome, so much the better. Others often commented that his connections seemed to know no bounds, and he considered this personal attribute one of the main reasons for his success.

In the early days, things had been much simpler. He and his wife Marnie had built a business that could no longer be considered small. Fortune Consolidated Industries—FCI—was an entity that the Fortune family was rightfully proud to wholly own and operate. It incorporated just about every aspect of the food service sector with farming, production, distribution, wholesale and retail all part of the big picture. It was a huge enterprise, requiring his constant attention.

Thinking back, he was amazed at how it had grown. He would often joke to his wife that things were really getting out of hand.

"How did the two of us get this lucky?" he would tease.

It hadn't always been easy, and with the ebb and flow of the economy in the past 50-plus years, some years were very good and sometimes it had been necessary to batten down the hatches, as Dan's father Fletcher had termed those periods when staying in business was the main business objective.

FCI had started out as Fortune's Family Market, a minor grocery storefront in the small town where Dan had grown up. It was originally Fletcher's. The late Fletcher Fortune was something of a local legend, with a reputation for hard work, hard living and working others as hard as he could get away with. Many locals had their own stories of "Double F" as he was called, not all of them complimentary.

Dan was the eldest of two sons, and he and his father had not always seen eye to eye. There had been many battles growing up. Dan's own sense of fairness didn't mesh well with Fletcher's equally adamant stance on getting the edge on every relationship he had in life, whether it was with his employees, neighbors or family. "My old man could squeeze the last dollar out of any situation, but that trait cost him so much more," Dan would lament.

In the '60s, Dan jumped at the chance to get away from his roots. His anticipated direction was a law degree and then hopefully to catch on with a law firm in the city, make partner and visit his hometown only during holidays.

Blessed with an equal balance of academic ability and athleticism, Dan had managed to win a small scholarship and settled into trying to experience campus life to its fullest and get that education. He made his university hockey team after a walk on tryout.

Dan had never felt so alive in his young life. After initially joining the Screaming Eagles, as the school team was known, he worked himself into the role of 1st line center. The coaching staff had started giving him increasing responsibility on the ice, which spilled over into the dressing room and practices. He was becoming a leader and strived to set a good example for his teammates. For all the strife Dan had with his father, one thing was certain: he had been indelibly imprinted with a work ethic that somewhat awed others his age. Dan decided they couldn't possibly understand what it was like to grow up in a small town with depression-era parents who took nothing in life for granted, when he thought back on an existence that he had every intention of leaving far behind.

Just before the playoffs in his first season, the university athletics director was waiting for him as he came off the ice after practice and asked to speak privately. Something was definitely up, Dan thought. "Your mother needs you to call home," the AD blurted out. "It's your father."

When he called he could sense in his mother the trepidation that he had long associated with her approach to bad news. "Danny, you need to come home as soon as you can," she said quietly. "Your father has passed away ... and ...," Her voice broke, trailing away into unmistakable muffled sobs as Dan listened, unsettled, on the other end of the line.

"Is Pete there with you, Mom?" Dan asked. Peter Fortune was Dan's brother, younger by exactly one year. Peter wasn't likely to leave the comforts of home anytime soon. Dan often wondered if his brother's ambition would ever appear, if he would ever want to challenge himself, test his abilities against the world. What happened to the kid who wanted to race me to the bus stop every day? Oh well, it was good that Pete had hung in, as his mother was going to need him to lean on as she faced the future as a widow. Perhaps his brother would need to run the Market for a while until things cleared up a bit and they could decide what to do.

Dan hung up, promising to hurry back to his mother's side. He didn't realize it, but he was also heading back to what would eventually, though inadvertently, be a totally different life from the one he'd thought would be his just 20 minutes before.

At the funeral home, the three Fortunes met many who gathered to give support, as small towns do in these sorts of events. The smaller the town, the more meaningfully people treat a death and funerals anyway, Dan thought, even if there weren't a lot of reasons for people to be overly shocked or saddened by his father's passing. In greeting guests, he heard many rehashed stories of Double F, lots of them told before and all making him grimace inside.

After the service and the luncheon, an equally exhausted Dan, Peter and their mother retreated to the family home to discuss the last few days and think about the immense changes that Fletcher's passing away would bring to all of their lives. His mother related what she knew to Dan on Double F's last day.

Their father had seemed in reasonable spirits when he left for the Market that morning. The day would have started off with an early meeting at the request of some of the staff. They had approached him to discuss some of their concerns about salaries and working conditions. They were also concerned about the impact of a national grocery chain setting up in the larger community just down the road. Double F usually just avoided these kinds of meetings, seeing placating staff as a foolish waste of time. He figured he didn't need input on the business. It wasn't their names on the sign, he reasoned. Why should I listen to them? If they didn't like it, they could always go someplace else.

Evidently Fletcher Fortune had let the meeting get underway and then became quite upset with what he was hearing. Never one to pay too much attention to the nuances of communication, he declared that if everyone would just keep their heads down and plug along, all would be fine. He had started making motions to leave the room, considering the meeting complete.

He was held up, though, as the staff wasn't sure that all was well. They didn't share his outward air of confidence. To them, things were definitely reaching a crisis point. Exasperated, it wasn't long before his temper got the better of him. He rose up to rebut someone's point, but didn't quite get to his feet before he collapsed to the floor, dead on arrival. According to all present, there was no one to call but the coroner, as Double F had most definitely passed from this world.

"And as far as I know, that's what happened," his mother said, her eyes misting over. At that moment Mrs. Fortune was feeling too young to be widowed and alone. Moving past her story she regained her composure. "I want you both to go with me in the morning to meet with Mr. Press," his mother asked. "He said there was an urgent matter that needed to be addressed." Ashley Press was Fletcher's long-time lawyer and knew where most—no, make that all—of the skeletons Fletcher had buried were hidden or left bleaching in the sun somewhere, Dan mused.

Ashley Press was as old school as possible, and something in the way he had always conducted his relationship with Dan's father struck a younger Dan as unseemly and manipulative. Mr. Press had never held public office or any of the powers that often attracted people in small towns with a higher education and a thirst to be at the center of things.

Being an insider, though, was very attractive to Press, and the spoils that might be available to one whose sense of ethics weren't necessarily fully aligned with the greater good of the community often won over his decision-making. Dan had now decided, after sitting in on half a semester of pre-law, that he despised people like Ashley Press and all they stood for. But he knew he would go with his mother.

The next day Ashley gravely embraced Dan's mother, acknowledged Peter with a nod and then locked eyes with Dan. Perhaps he's wondering why he hasn't seen me around in a couple of months, Dan thought.

"Your father told me you'd left town to study law, Dan. What have you learned since you've been away? That the ways of the world can sometimes be a cruel mistress, I reckon," Mr. Press said.

Dan replied that, given the events of the past days, he wasn't quite sure what he could take away from his schooling so far, but that he was eager to stay at university and finish what he'd started. He couldn't help but notice that Press averted his eyes upon hearing Dan's answer. Early in Dan's life, Ashley Press had left the impression that he was the human equivalent of a large black crow. Angular and severe, Press was always similarly clad in one of several black suits he'd obtained in a much earlier era. His appearance reflected what Dan imagined were his views on the world: everyone and everything in their designated places and if those places were somewhat useful to him, so much the better.

"Well, let's get started," Ashley said to the ceiling as much as to anyone in the room. "There's a problem we have to address." Press continued, "Quite simply, I'm afraid Double F couldn't have died at a worse time for all of you. Unfortunately, I have found his estate is in a state of disarray, and once creditors and taxes are taken care of there won't be a lot left over."

"That can't be," said Dan's mother. "What about our saving and investments, our bonds—our house? What's to be left of my husband's estate?"

In Ashley's best impression of a full disclosure mode, he spoke to the family in chilling terms. "Your husband did the best he could, Mrs. Fortune, but you of all people would know that the Fortune Family Market hasn't had the necessary revenues in the last few years. Modernization and progress overtook some of Double F's business ideas, and many in this town have quietly been going over to the supermarket in the next town for better prices and what they saw as an enhanced overall operation. To be frank with all of you, the business was on borrowed time. Fletcher had pledged all of your assets against his operating debt. I looked after setting up the financing arrangement myself, and now this truly unfortunate turn of events has your creditors looking to foreclose. After a period of respect for the deceased, of course," he explained in a tone that, for a long time after, Dan would say left a coating of frost on his family and everything else in that office.

Not so Fast ...

Dan was angry with what he heard—angry at Ashley Press, but mostly angry with his father as he had not taken any precautions against what had happened. Yes, he had life insurance, but not enough, and the proceeds were already pledged against the debt. He looked to see his mother's and brother's reactions. Peter, passive as always, just sat there as if in a trance, his stone gaze staring squarely at the face of the large grandfather clock standing in the corner.

His mother looked horrified at what she'd just heard. Her relationship with her late husband had always been one of separate roles: his as the breadwinner trying to make the family business work and hers as a caregiver to their two sons. How they both went about those roles was not considered the domain of the other and was certainly not looked at with any great sense of insight. With his sons, Fletcher Fortune meted out punishment if it was needed but often didn't have the slightest clue what the transgression was. Dan always felt his father based his decisions about what was necessary on the kind of day he was having, and his lack of empathy toward just about everyone he dealt with day to day ultimately became his family environment.

Dan hadn't thought about his parents' relationship that much and had often viewed his mother in a rather benign light. She'd been there in her own quiet way to make sure everyone's needs were met. She was a product of her age and geography; entertaining dreams of a different life wasn't in any way part of her makeup.

Post-war, people had just headed back to what and who they knew. Life was simple, and they didn't pay much attention to a rapidly changing and wider world where cities were growing and ambitions were being met. His mother would not have troubled herself with the family financial picture, and making changes to it wasn't what she knew or cared to know.

"Boys, I'm going to need your help," Mother said finally after everyone had absorbed the shock of Mr. Press's disclosure.

Dan sat there wishing he could have been anywhere else and weighed his family's diminishing options. He looked to Peter and then back to his mother, seeing his own dreams spiralling down the drain, scholarship or not. If there was to be a solution it had to come from him—of that much he was sure.

He remembered a conversation with a high school classmate he'd once had. Beth, who was two or three years older than him, lived close enough that they would often walk to school together if they saw each other on the road. She had an older boyfriend who attended the same high school but had graduated to a life on the family farm. Dan certainly wasn't into girls at that stage, but he always considered his conversations with Beth to be a bit of an education into people and things. When they arrived at school and headed to their respective classes, he always felt the time had passed too quickly.

People and things—Dan had a natural curiosity for those two areas which, when you thought of it, covered quite a lot of ground. When Dan had questions about life, he could always count on Beth for a reasonable answer that seemed well thought out even though she explained them so simply.

Beth worked for his father part time and generally steady in summers and during school breaks. Dan asked her once what she wanted out of life. She told him she had put aside almost all the money she'd earned at the Market and was hoping to get a college nursing diploma and then work at the regional hospital, probably in emergency, as that seemed like it had a lot of action.

He thought about the last conversation he'd had with Beth, on the Friday just before spring break in Beth's graduating year. He saw her on the road ahead and ran to catch up. He noticed her moving faster as he got closer, as if she was avoiding him. When he caught up, he reached out to touch her shoulder as she might not have known it was him behind her. He could tell she was crying as she quickly tried to wipe away the tears.

"What's the matter, Beth?" he asked.

"I can't say, but we won't be walking to school anymore," was her reply.

"Why not?"

"Danny, you're a nice boy, but sometimes you ask too many questions," she said and she looked away so he couldn't meet her eyes. He fell in beside her and they continued the walk in silence. He felt like she wanted to say something but couldn't start and he made several comments on the budding trees and about how the earth was coming back to life after the long winter. He had just launched into how some of the town's first robins of spring had made themselves known when she stopped abruptly and said, "Dan, shut up please!"

"There's something I need to say. I found out from Dr. Sloan that I'm pregnant," she sobbed. "This isn't what we planned and I can't believe that I could have been so stupid to let this happen. There were so many things I wanted to do before I settled down."

In the last five years, Dan had lost touch with Beth but had heard that, after a rushed wedding, she and her husband had brought first one, then two more children into the world. Later on he'd seen her while helping at the Market. She was shopping with her children and he felt somehow unsure about approaching her. Instead, he observed her and the kids through the plexi-glass of the swing doors leading to the "employees only" area. Although they weren't that far apart in age, Beth appeared much older now and had lost the carefree image she had always projected. He could tell she adored her children, though, and was just dealing with her circumstances the best she could.

Mr. Press's stern voice interrupted his reverie as he asked Dan's mother if she would require him to handle the dispersal of Fortune's assets to settle the estate. His mother started to reply when Dan found his own voice and stated simply, "No, Mr. Press, we won't be needing you or your services. Furthermore, my sense is that there has been some mismanagement by you in your service to my father."

Mr. Press's eyes narrowed as he looked over his glasses and across his large old desk. "What would you know about these types of matters? Or has a partial semester at university given you all kinds of insights into the workings of business, finance and law?" he asked.

Dan's mother stood up as if to intervene. "Dan, Mr. Press, please. I have buried a husband this week and I don't care to hear an argument right now."

Dan understood and rose to leave, but his final glance at Press could not be interpreted as anything but malice. This case wasn't closed, and the older man would regret both his actions and his comments one day. As he pushed through the door and left through the outer office, he heard his mother say, "Good day, Mr. Press." Outside the law office, Dan turned on his mother and brother and said, loud enough for passersby to overhear, "I can't believe that man and what he has done to us. How could father have been that naive and trusting?" His mother shushed him all the way back to the car and the trio went home in absolute and dreadful silence.

Pulling the Plug

This faded memory still pained Dan and he returned to the present with an unconscious shudder when he felt Marnie grab his shoulders from behind and start to knead them. "What are you thinking about, honey?" she asked.

"Oh nothing really, just the old days, I guess," he replied. Marnie hated that response and started to reply but then decided she wouldn't. She knew Dan had come from a tough place in making FCI what it was today and early on, circumstances had been overwhelmingly stacked against him. Granted, they had done it together and she knew her spouse would tell anybody who wanted to listen that he and Marnie had created their success as a team. It was just that she felt her husband carried around way too much baggage from his upbringing and she resented that some of that baggage had found its way into their own family. She knew from her short-lived former professional background that Dan often showed signs of anxiety that were slowly but surely insinuating themselves into the way he related to her, his children and those at FCI who had helped make it a success. She worked with him as subtly as possible to get him to think about passing on the torch at FCI so they could withdraw into a happy and active retirement for them both.

However, she couldn't escape the feeling that she and Dan were at some sort of crossroad. She couldn't yet put a finger on exactly what needed to be done and when. She had to find a way to gain some clarity and perspective. She didn't want to make this thing more messed up than it was, a dark picture rising in her mind of the potential of financial ruin for her family. She thought it would kill them both to see what they'd worked so hard to create come tumbling down. Marnie feared the bitter vetch of failure as strongly as her husband did.

She also knew that, appearance-wise, not one of their friends or business contacts would guess at the turmoil the Fortune family and FCI were facing. Our front shop looks fabulous, but our back shop is anything but, she thought, and will eventually betray us if we don't get a proper handle on our situation. Worry lines creased her face as she considered all the factors at play. Boy, she thought, it sure would be good if Dad were still around to help guide me on this one.

Marnie remembered a saying that her own father, a family physician, had often said to her and her sisters when they couldn't agree on something.

"Girls, a house divided against itself cannot stand." Then he would say, in his calm kindly voice, "Now how might we resolve our problems here?"

Marnie's father, Dr. Olaf Farver, had come from Denmark as a teenager with his family. She smiled as she thought back to him and how he had always loved old quotes, especially those he could pull out of his readings and notes on historically notable people and events and apply them to family instances. He had passed away just nine years before, after a life of service to many prominent citizens of the city where she lived before leaving to make a future with Dan. She missed her father every day and particularly now with what she could see bearing down on them on the horizon.

One of the most important things she had learned from her father was that once the question—any question—was asked, it was very impolite, even impolitic, to finish the question and not listen to the answer, or worse, abruptly follow your question with your own answer. It was a sure way to turn a simple conflict into an all-out war, he'd said. And besides, it was just plain rude.

"Give those who are questioned the space they need to forge an answer," he would always remind his daughters. "It's your measure of respect for others that you will listen to their point of view, which is often quite workable in helping to gain a lasting agreement that works for all. Remember, girls, none of us is as smart as all of us." All of his ways of approaching challenges, conflicted opinions and personalities came flooding back to her.

She often reminisced with her children that he had a way with his patients that not only capably treated their physical conditions but paid close attention to their mental states, as he had come to realize that the two were closely linked and indivisible. "Girls, I have treated a lot of people for physical conditions that started out as mental conditions like stress and personal dysfunction. There are a lot of people out there who, if they could get out of their own way, wouldn't need half the prescriptions I write."

Marnie's mother had died much too young, when she and her sisters were just school-aged girls. Dr. Farver had carried on alone, never remarrying, always focused on turning out proper young women with careers of their own, to insulate them from marriages that he feared might be unequal unions.

Marnie had felt for some time that FCI's professional managers and the next generation of the Fortune family could and should be handling the day-to-day operational issues and that she and Dan needed to gracefully and correctly hand over the reins, stepping back to provide sober second thought, only when necessary.

Marnie returned to her cottage study from the porch and now it was her turn to retreat fully into her thoughts. She and Dan both used this quiet space, but they both realized it was more her space than his. When her husband got to the cottage or any of their other properties, he spent most of his time engaged in projects. To Dan, as long as an activity had a tangible outcome and he'd made an improvement, he felt it was a worthwhile use of his time.

Marnie's daydream continued as she thought about how she and Dan had met. She entered the picture after Dan had decided to drop out of school and return to the town to try and save Fortune's Family Market from the clutches of its creditors, led by his father's former trusted advisor. Dan had come back to school after a week off to decide his future.

He met quickly with the dean and the head of his dorm to let them know he'd decided to leave. Both realized that remarkable young men usually stay remarkable as their lives progress, as long as they get the right kind of direction in those years when they're still open to fresh thinking and different ideas. Knowing Dan's desire for a future in corporate law, they both asked him to reconsider, but his mind was made up and his sense of duty to his family was clear to him.

He quickly said goodbye. After dropping by the arena to see his teammates and wish them luck in what remained of the season, he strode out to his father's, or what was now his car. Glumly, Dan started loading it up with the contents of his room.

He always told Marnie in later years that as downcast as he was, he couldn't help but notice a very pretty coed wearing glasses, reading a book under a tree on the campus lawn by herself. He'd felt that he might as well have been invisible, as she seemed held in rapt attention by whatever she was reading, not seeing his sidelong glances as he loaded up. He finished stowing his things in the car and thought to himself, "Well I won't be seeing any girl that gorgeous where I'm headed," and jumped into the driver's seat and turned the ignition key.

He had initially hoped to make the three-and-a-half hour drive back to town and get a good night's sleep so he could get into the Market early. This day, though, had a few surprises left in it. The first one was decidedly unpleasant, as his car wouldn't start. It would turn over but just couldn't get ignition. He tried a few times and then hopped out to lift the hood. He stared at it for several minutes, trying to remember how the mechanics at the repair shop solved issues like this.

"It's your distributor cap, you know." He was so wrapped up in his mechanical issues that he failed to realize that the free advice coming from behind him was from the girl reading the book. When he turned, he noticed she wasn't making eye contact and appeared still caught up with what was on the pages.

"How do you know that, and what do you know about cars?" he asked.

"Well, I know by the sound your car is making," she said, her green eyes now peering over the book to focus on him. "My Dad's car does this from time to time and he just makes sure the main wire is snug before anything else. I would try that if I were you."

Well what do you know? This lovely bookworm is also a specialist in cars, he thought, laughing inside. What a day!

"Can you fix it?" he said, thinking that this situation was as unreal as the last couple of weeks had been for him.

The girl dropped her book and got up from the grass. She came over to the car and said, "My name is Marnie and you are...?"

"Dan Fortune," he responded, taking her outstretched hand to shake.

"Well, Dan Fortune, I can tell from here that your main distributor cord is your problem," and she reached down, easily putting it in place. "Now jump in and see if that works." The engine quickly came to life and Dan popped back out to thank her.

"Hey, your name sounds familiar to me. You aren't the Dan Fortune that's on the hockey team, are you?"

"I was," he told her. With a sigh, he explained that he was dropping out and he told her the events of the last few weeks that had led to this decision.

"Oh, that's a shame and I'm sorry to hear about your loss. Our team will miss you as well. I think we were one quality center from the nationals."

This girl continued to simply amaze him; a hockey fan and mechanically inclined. He wondered if she was an heiress to a brewery as well. Coming to his senses, he quickly asked if he could at least buy her a coffee for helping him out.

"Sure you can," she replied quickly.

The initial impromptu date was a complete success and Dan didn't leave the city for several hours, arriving home after midnight. They talked about everything and anything and they both felt good as they said good night. He would make the journey into the city for three more years until Marnie finished her psychology degree.

Later, after her graduation ceremony, he spoke with her father to see whether he had any objections to Dan's intention to ask Marnie to marry him. "Dan," her father replied, "all of my daughters are very special to me and I'm glad that the two of you found one another. I believe a good relationship means that the two people coming together can add a lot to each other's lives. In essence, a successful relationship means that one and one no longer equal two but some continually higher number beyond the sum of its parts. Each adds value to the other and together you become a powerful force." He paused then continued, "You and my daughter have that opportunity but it's something that needs to be worked at. To be blessed with that multiplier effect is something that requires a commitment to communication."

Marnie smiled at the memory and wondered if he had ever thought about how a cord could come loose when a car was parked.

Dan at the Helm

It was early on a Saturday and the summer's heat was just starting to build on what was promising to be a hot day. Dan pulled into the Market, parked at the far end and walked toward the building. His mind drifted to what had occurred over the past year since he'd come back to manage the family business.

His first action had been to take down all the signs for reserved staff parking, and the last post to come out was the one for Double F. He'd heard that this action had caused a few of the staff to comment; they didn't think it made sense for the owner to be making the long walk from the back of the lot.

Baffled by this bit of back-hall chatter, he bitterly thought, Owner? Owner of what? A rickety old building that needed a new roof, a parking lot that requiring paving, a tired interior and bad supplier relationships? Ooh ... lucky me. On top of that, a town consumer base that preferred to drive 20 clicks out of town and shop at the new Super Mart. They are kicking my ass and slowly crushing us, he thought.

The walk up from the back always let him clear his head and gave him a perspective on how his customers saw Fortune Family Market. This day he took note that a coat of paint on the girders supporting the awning across the front should find its way on to the action list. So could calling the shopping cart supplier and seeing about some refurbished buggies. And they were also going to have to get the local pigeons to roost elsewhere. There's a new sheriff in town, he thought, and customers shouldn't have to dodge pigeon droppings.

Fortune's Impasse

The period following his father's death was very busy for him. His father's passing away had put Dan on a very short leash with his bank. The debt is going to kill us if we don't get some relief, he thought. I'll just have to somehow drive more revenue through the Market, he decided, but how?

Dan was starting to experience significant stress in his life for the first time. The brinksmanship of meeting the biweekly payroll was almost crippling when he thought about that. Those thoughts always came in the night when he would wake up in a sweat. He found it maddening to find himself awake at exactly the same time on his bedside clock: 3:45 in the morning. He didn't know it at the time but he was experiencing the early stages of a self-reinforcing sleep pattern caused by stressful situations. He would experience this at various times throughout his life, though, for some strange reason, it would improve for long stretches, even years at a time. He would relapse when things started to bother him, and often found the only answer was to get up for the day. Back in those days, this was a common scenario, and many of the early shift employees would find the employee access door open with Dan working in the store, his extended workday launched hours before.

There was no doubt his family's other creditors were still hovering, biding their time, waiting to see the business topple. The fact was, they thought Dan would probably have made a few positive changes to the building itself before the inevitable foreclosure, so why not let him play with it for a while.

Certainly the Market had grim prospects but, soon after taking the reins, Dan had decided he wasn't going to give anyone the satisfaction of seeing it go under and have his family go through the humiliation of a failed enterprise. Besides, he thought, even if many were driving over to the new competitor, there were many others in the town who were less mobile who counted on his store to remain open, and he wasn't going to let anyone down.

He had let two of his father's key employees go soon after coming back. They were both entrenched in some of his father's old ways and management practices. As in countless changing of the guard circumstances in a business, there are always some who look to the new regime as a breath of fresh air, and an opportunity to define themselves in the renewed situation. But there are also others who cling to old practices, procedures and standards. No matter what is done to appease them, they cannot and will not, allow progress to happen.

One was the meat manager, the other the Market's original female employee, who was the head cashier and bookkeeper. Dan decided to make the change to try and gain the confidence of his remaining employees, as the two he dismissed were known to be quite resistant to any changes in roles and responsibilities. Besides, he decided, it would help get his payroll in line and he would just have to assume their responsibilities for the immediate future and try to right the ship.

Then something fortunate happened. Actually three things happened and they occurred within days of each other.

The first appeared in the guise of a rather plain and unassuming young woman in her late teens who came striding into the store. At that point in her life, those who knew her best would have described Rebekah Jean Cameron as severe. She carried herself in a way that said she was not to be trifled with.

She purposely navigated the aisles of the store until she found her target. She gave Dan Fortune a pressing nudge on his back to get his attention, exhibiting a solidness he would later come to understand and appreciate. He'd been pricing some canned fruit tins and for the fourth time that week had received a nasty paper cut from the wax paper ribbon that trailed out of his labelling gun.

Squelching a choice curse word, he turned quickly, finger to his mouth, and immediately recognized in his visitor the family resemblance to an old school friend, Pudge Cameron. Pudge had been the starting center on the District High School football team every year he'd been enrolled, which was at least six years, if Dan's memory served correctly. He was the anchor of the offensive line—heck, Pudge was an offensive line.

Before Rebekah could introduce herself, Dan said, "You're a Cameron, aren't you? Has anyone ever told you you're the spitting image of your brother?" he said, laughing.

"Yes, just about everyone who knows him, but it usually doesn't start things off very well," Rebekah shot back.

Rebekah Cameron was noted for a forwardness that most people might find intimidating. For example, she wouldn't make any kind of formal application for a job before first deciding if she could work with the boss. So far, Dan hadn't passed muster. She also preferred to be known by the decidedly unladylike "RJ," which she noted was easier to remember.

"Dan, I came in to talk with you. I think I can help you." She was ready to launch into what she thought help looked like, but Dan was still thinking about her older brother, and his people side came out.

"Well, I always thought a lot of Pudge," he reflected. "He's a great guy. I haven't seen him in a while." Dan paused before asking "What's he doing these days?" hoping the answer was something good. You just didn't know with Pudge.

"Didn't you hear he bought the McDougall property?" she answered. Continuing, she told Dan all about the move Pudge had made to start his own small hog production farm, and so far things were going his way. The feed and care of the pigs was everything to producing the end product, which was the best pork in the area. His plan was to branch into beef and lamb as well, but that was a longer-term objective and, as she said, "Who knows if it'll all work out?"

"Your store should be stocking his meat. He's still a little shy so he might not come to you himself, but I think more people would be drawn to you with some premium quality meat in here. I'm helping him out when I can," she said, now warming to the discussion. "Another reason I came by is I've heard a bit about what you've gone through with the store and I think you could use my help."

"Oh? What would you like to do around here? Are you all through with school?" he asked.

"Well, what needs doing? I'm sure there are trucks to unload, customer requests to respond to, shelves to stock and pricing to be done, although hopefully without the blood loss, she said, smiling and looking down at the cuts on Dan's hands. I could also help you by making sure we get their money before they leave if you need me on the front end," was her response.

Dan liked this young woman. "You sound like a Swiss army knife, Rebekah. That covers most of what we do here."

She held out her hand to Dan. "And by the way, yes, I finished high school. Our parents don't have a lot and so more schooling at this point is out of the question and I know what I want out of life. So does that mean I'm hired?"

Dan checked his kneejerk response which was to say yes, but couldn't hold out in the end beneath RJ's intense gaze. After a short pause he replied, "Well, yeah then, I guess it does. I could use some bodies here, but the situation is a tough one. I don't know that I could afford to pay you that much."

"You have a pretty good reputation, Dan. Everyone knows you've been up against it with the situation with your father and all …. I'm sure you'll be fair with me now and if it works out you'll be fair with me afterwards."

He would soon find out ambition and an up-front, in-your-face style was her calling card. And with that brief encounter and subsequent hire, Dan made what he would later realize was his first great business decision.

Another Shoe Drops

It is said that bad things, such as celebrity deaths, come in threes, but if you pay close attention, good things often happen that way as well.

The second piece of good fortune that came Dan's way happened just over a week after RJ had started working in the Market. Dan had been duly impressed by her work ethic and noticed that she cheerfully took on any task that needed to be done and was competent both behind the scenes and at the front end of working life at the Market.

Observing her helping unload a truck one day had been a revelation. The driver from the produce supplier and Dan's brother Peter were sending cases of product down the rollers out of the trailer as fast as they could, and RJ was stacking them with time and energy to spare. As he often did, Dan had come back to help out but by the time he arrived the order had been offloaded.

He was just about to sign off on the bill of lading for the shipment when he heard, "Uh-oh. Don't sign that, Dan. We have a problem." She had opened one of the boxes of lettuce to find some of the heads with a less-than-market-fresh look to them. She grabbed one of the more wilted heads and advanced on the driver.

"What are you trying to deliver to us?" she asked with a look that told the driver he might be force-fed the greens if he didn't come up with some sort of explanation. With Dan in her peripheral vision she faced the unfortunate man with a gaze that was all icy vehemence. "This won't do for Fortune Family Markets, my friend." Turning back to the stacked boxes, she told the driver and Peter to help her look through the remainder of the shipment to check it. In the end she found 18 of 30 boxes were in various states of decay.

Interrupting the terrified man's protests that he was only the driver, RJ said, "Here's what you're going to do for us. First, I want whoever runs your company to give Mr. Fortune or myself a call to explain your firm's quality standards because those standards let us all down today. These look like they were picked a week ago. Second, you're going to load these cases back on that truck, go back, get us replacements and be back here stat. That's good, right? Oh and when we're happy, we'll pay for this shipment and not before that." The offending cases were loaded back onto the truck. Eyeing RJ cautiously, the driver edged away toward the cab of the truck, nodding, and drove away.

Dan watched all this unfold more as a spectator than a participant and shook his head. He was just starting to feel like he could put a mental framework around making the Market a better business, and in his heart he knew that the foundation of his vision would be on building out from himself; one day the business would require a nucleus of passionate people. He realized that RJ was going to be part of that and that she had the personality to push things forward. It might even help Peter, he thought.

"Uhh ... good job, RJ, but its Fortune Family *Market*, not *Markets*," he murmured, thinking she was already out of earshot. RJ had moved on with Peter to get the good portion of the shipment uncrated and out to the counter.

"Well, it will never be 'Markets' if we don't start making sure the people of this town get the very best we can be provide to them and their families. It won't even be 'Market'," came her loud, sharp retort as it volleyed across the produce counters toward his back. Dan noticed several shoppers look up with a start.

Knowing she was right, but smarting from her aggressive way, he thought of rounding back on her and reminding the brash younger woman just who was boss. He continued to stare away from her, pretending to look at the time clock and thinking better of making this conversation bigger than it needed to be. He smiled inwardly and thought, well she's as tough as nails but she's a keeper.

Seeing that he wasn't needed, Dan walked back up to the front just in time to see one of the cashiers pointing him out to a tall, well-dressed man who didn't seem to be there to shop. Dan was fairly certain he'd never laid eyes on this man in his life. He approached and the gentleman held out his hand. At that time, Dan was all of 22 years old. He noted that the other man looked more mature, established and very comfortable in his own skin, seemingly surrounded in an aura of intelligence and success.

"Hello, you must be Dan Fortune. I'm Ben Curtis," he said, and he took Dan's hand in his own, giving it a firm shake. Dan quickly sized him up as probably a salesman and expected he would soon proffer up something like a new brand of toothpaste with a point-of-purchase display for the front end of the store. Dan was wrong, though, and it turned out that the second good thing was about to happen.

Ben started to speak in a casual, yet direct way. "Dan, my in-laws live here in town and shop here in your store. Perhaps you know them, the Davises?"

Dan paused for a moment and before too long thought he could place both of them. "Your father-in-law always buys a roll of Life Savers, doesn't he? And his wife is here quite a lot. Yes, I know them. Great customers and nice people."

"That's them," Ben replied. "I married their daughter Ginny back a few years, and so we come to town with the little ones from time to time to see Grandpa and Grandma. We were short on hotdog buns for lunch and I was sent to retrieve some."

To Dan, Curtis seemed a little too dressed up for a hotdog picnic.

Sensing Dan's appraisal, he said, "I'm also in town to look at an investment opportunity for our family business. I have a meeting in about 20 minutes.

My father-in-law has been watching your business a little more closely than you may realize. Mr. Davis—er, Doug—is interested in investing in your operation here, Dan. He's seen the changes you've made and realizes that you aren't done. He admires the headway he sees you trying to make and is particularly impressed with you." He dropped his voice slightly and added, "Doug filled me in on what happened with your father's passing away and all."

Dan realized that he probably also knew about the financial pressures the Market was under as it seemed everyone tied into the business sector in town knew the story. Dan thought better of denying any problems existed as he sensed that Ben Curtis was sincere, and he decided to hear him out.

"Do you eat lunch, Dan?" Ben asked.

"Yeah, I eat lunch," Dan wearily replied.

"Well, why don't you come by the house and listen to my father-in-law? Who knows? You two might be a fit."

So Dan and Mr. Davis met over a hotdog for lunch that day, and several days later he was asked back. Mr. Davis was willing to be a silent partner in the Market for up to an eight-year period. He told Dan this was a midterm investment for him and that the buyout at the end and the cash flow during the term were what made sense for him. He offered Dan a good financial package, one that allowed Dan freedom in several areas. With a twinkle in his eye, Mr. Davis remarked that he needed to make sure the town's food supply stayed solvent and that he was investing in a person as much as a business.

"I think this works for both of us, Dan. I'm older and I don't like risk, so I like the fact that I can see what's going on with my money every time I drop in."

The arrangement would allow Dan to get out from under the creditors fronted by Ashley Press, and his savings on that outstanding debt alone would save him significant cash flow. His relationship with his banker would of course remain, as the bank provided an overdraft for the operating needs of the Market. He had recently found that the banker had started to become a little more like an ally and less of a watchdog. The tide was turning.

More importantly, his relationship with Doug Davis gave Dan the mental space he needed at that point to look at the Market less like his personal anchor and more like a sail that could potentially be filled with some wind and take him into a better future.

Just after his father had passed away and he'd come back to town to run the Market for his family, someone had commented to him that what he was trying to do could be done but it was going to take a lot of courage and conviction. *If you're the captain of a ship, it's never easy to climb into the crow's nest in the midst of a storm* ... was how he recalled the man putting it. He often thought about that analogy during the first year as he sought to gain the initial clarity about his future.

The freedom brought by the arrangement with Doug Davis allowed Dan to get better rest, run a better business and—most importantly—make better decisions that eventually started to make all the difference in the world.

You can't really plan to meet a lifelong friend, he thought. It just happens. If you're a good friend to others, the law of reciprocal behavior dictates that you'll usually get that in return. Before Dan had assumed control of the Market, he'd enjoyed some good friendships throughout his life. He didn't have a best friend, but he had many great friends, and the gang he ran with shared a lot of good experiences. Dan had been somewhat of a casualty in more ways than one when his life had changed so abruptly and he had to leave the campus life behind. Unfortunately most of those old relationships had withered and ceased when those who went away to colleges and universities met new people and shared new experiences. Communications back then made those early friendships almost impossible to maintain into adulthood.

He resigned himself for the time being to a strict focus on his business and just gave up on a social life other than seeing Marnie whenever he could make the drive to the city to visit her.

Dan considered himself a "people before anything else" person, and though he enjoyed the give and take with some of the Market's staff, it felt a little forced and the invisible line between them became apparent most days. Over time he came to know the Market's regulars better. There was a slowly but steadily growing group that he was immensely grateful to for favoring him and the Market with their business.

There are fates much worse than mine, he decided. Besides, he appreciated getting to know Mr. Davis and having his friendship and advice. Dan soon came to see him as a source of reasonable advice and a suitable sounding board on some of the issues that came up. He often jokingly referred to his senior silent partner as "the senator," and he knew that Mr. Davis didn't entirely dislike the title.

Still, they were 44 years apart in age; further yet even than Double F and Dan had been. There were just some reference points between Mr. Davis and himself on which the generation gap would never be bridged. He had never felt close to his father, but by the end of that first year in the store he felt at least he finally understood him better. There were some things about running that type of business that weren't readily explainable to an outsider.

Later that first year, in one of his discussions with Mr. Davis, the older man mentioned his son-in-law, Ben. "Do you ever get to the city, Dan? I think it would be a good idea for you to become better acquainted with Ben. He's a good man and makes things happen."

"Yes, he seems like he has it all together, that's for sure," Dan responded. He'd thought sometimes about Ben since that day they'd met and realized that they'd never really talked beyond having lunch at the Davis's.

"I know he would enjoy hearing from you. Ben comes from very fortunate family circumstances, Dan. They're a large, well connected, remarkable business clan and have enjoyed a lot of success, but they're an even more remarkable family. Seeing what he's creating with our Virginia and the kids now, Mrs. Davis and I are so happy they got together. Go see him, Dan."

"Well, there is this girl that I go over to see when I can," Dan said. "I usually head up on Sunday and spend the day. Do you think Ben would have time this coming weekend?"

"We're calling over to wish their eldest a happy birthday tonight. Young Kevin turned eight years old today," said Mr. Davis, beaming. "I'll tee it up for the two of you. I think you should get to know each other better. Who knows what you might get started between you."

And that was the third leg on the stool of good happenstance. Ben would become a lifelong friend and mentor, who would show Dan what his destiny could really look like.

Ben's Big Idea

"Daan Fortuuune, pick up on line #1. Daan Fortuuune, please pickup on line #1." Dan smiled, as he always did at the way Ethel spoke into the microphone over the store public address system. The muffled sound of her voice made it sound like she couldn't decide whether to speak into the mic or eat it.

Ethel was a holdover from the Double F days and had been with the Market since before Dan was born. She was no longer that effective and resisted some of the newer developments in the industry. But she was another employee that had Dan's back at all times and acted as a mother hen to them all.

The Market was approaching its fourth year under Dan's leadership and the operation continued to generate buzz in the community and move its weekly numbers ever higher. Slow to build out his team, he was involving RJ and Peter in some of the supplier relationships. However, at this point, most calls were still for him, so when he heard the squawk of the PA kick in, he instinctively moved from where he was to one of the three phone stations.

Thinking he'd caught Ethel's line of sight from the raised office on the front end, he motioned with a hand to his ear that he would be taking the call in the meat department. Picking up the handset, he said, "Thank you for calling Fortune's. This is Dan."

"How you been keeping, stranger? Long time no talk." Dan heard the exuberant voice of his friend Ben Curtis coming down the phone line over

Fortune's Impasse

the din of the meat cutters plying their trade and fighting the daily battle of keeping the refrigerated counters full.

Over top of the racket, Dan cringed when he heard Ethel again paging "Daan Fortuuune, pick up on line #1. Daan Fortuuune, please pick up on line #1." Due to her questionable eyesight and an out-of-date glasses prescription, Ethel had missed seeing Dan go to the phone. The Market's phones were outdated and there was no way of seeing that he was now on the line.

What the hell? Ethel?

"Hang on a minute please, Ben." Holding his composure and his hand over the handset receiver he called down the cereal aisle to a young part timer who was warily eying a teetering skid of product in need of unboxing and pricing for sale on the store shelves. "Timmy, can you run up and tell her I got it?" Dan yelled, not totally frustrated with Ethel but clearly heading in that direction. "Thanks, Buddy," he called after the boy and went back to his call.

"Ben Curtis, it's great to hear from you. What's up?" Dan was direct with his answer. He tended to mask his sense of urgency in friendly terms. It wasn't that he didn't want to speak with his friend. It was just that these days the Market was so busy with quite a few unfamiliar customers driving in from neighboring towns and pushing the whole staff and his store's capacity to the limit.

"Dan, I know you're busy. I just wanted to tell you I'm coming into town tonight to see the folks and wondered if we could get together."

"Of course, but I have to tell you, Ben, I'm going to stay after hours and work on a few things here, so the doors will be locked. Knock hard on the front window and I'll let you in. Can we meet here?"

"Absolutely," said Ben. "Look for me around 7ish. We'll have a coffee and talk. I hope you stock Sanka," he said, laughing. "Ginny encourages me to drink only decaf later in the day. Says it will actually help me sleep better."

"She's right," Dan confirmed. "Boy, everyone's thinking healthy these days. Believe it or not, our plain-cut cigarettes are now being outsold by filtered!" Knowing that they could talk later, they signed off.

Dan hung up the phone and glanced over to see RJ, who had jumped in with Timmy to finish stocking the cereals. He couldn't help but notice the young teen was staring straight ahead at his task and nodding his head with a little too much animation at everything RJ said. She was enforcing some thinking she had about how to do the task more quickly, while still making room for shoppers and their carts trying to navigate their way around them. Dan didn't know if he was learning and retaining her instructions or was just scared to death of her.

RJ had developed into that cross-functional employee that Dan had needed at Fortune's. She could be counted on to do most anything that needed to be done, as Dan had originally anticipated. He hadn't yet given her any sort of formal title, but those who worked in the store acknowledged that she had special status and had evolved into the second in command in every aspect of the business.

RJ's main area of weakness was her people skills. She was decisive and preferred that Dan be decisive as well. He could sense that his second in command experienced significant stress if he wavered on a judgment call. Though they possessed similar traits, they didn't see eye to eye on everything. Overall it worked well if he deployed her skills in the right way. He received feedback from Peter and others that RJ was at times so opinionated she had difficulty letting others participate in resolving problems.

She often just cleared everyone out and did the task herself to ensure that it was completed to her own high standards. The result, though, was that she could be so direct with the other staff that sometimes she alienated them.

Dan still played pickup hockey with a group on Wednesday afternoons and likened RJ to a player that was supremely talented but also a bit of a puck hog, trying to skate through the opposing team but with decidedly mixed results.

Dan pondered this problem and had decided that talking to RJ about this was long past due, but every time he went to discuss it with her, he found himself blanching at the thought of her reaction. Yes, he thought, I'm going to have a long talk with her but not today.

Avoiding RJ and Timmy, he walked to the far side of the five-aisle store, deciding instead to take a walk around the whole place to see if everything was shipshape for Ben's visit. Dan figured that everyone who owned and operated a business always hoped to be at his or her best when fellow entrepreneurs were in, even just for a visit.

Rounding through the aisles, he made a list of a few areas for those on shift to attend to. Then he headed out through the newly installed automatic door to the parking lot, where he started to pick up the odd stray pieces of litter that had escaped his scrutiny when he'd walked across the parking lot that morning.

Dan had absolutely fallen in love with the business and couldn't imagine himself doing anything else now, even considering himself fortunate to be getting a real-life working education instead of the life he had once sought.

The Market's performance for the last year had allowed him to start funding a small nest egg for his mother to live on. She would probably never get over the shock of his father's passing away and the financial anxiety wrought through that experience. However, she could now afford to get involved in the town's lawn bowling league and in the winter months take part in some of the bonspiels put on over at the community's curling club.

Some of the more well-to-do people her age now called themselves "snowbirds" and were starting to spend a few weeks of the winter in Florida to escape the weather. Dan's mother never mentioned wanting to go, and he guessed she probably felt it didn't reflect her lifestyle to lay out money for such frivolous trips. She wouldn't feel good about being away from him and Peter for that long anyway, Dan decided.

Late that day, he welcomed Ben into the store and they sat in his small office sipping coffee and chatting about what they both had going on. Then Ben paused and their discussion came to a halt. Dan had come to know that the look on Ben's face meant it was time to get down to the real reason for his visit. Over the last few years, Dan and Ben had seen each other every few months, mostly when he was in the city to see Marnie and sometimes when Ben came to town.

His father-in-law was still invested in Dan and the Fortune Family Market, their eight-year payout on the loaned principal doing not just what it was originally intended to do but doing even better. Mr. Davis was pleased to be able to participate in the larger-than-anticipated earnings that the business was providing. Such was his original faith in Dan that he had insisted the deal that they structured be weighted in favor of their mutual success. The agreement stated that should the business experience the best-case scenario of their three projected cash flow budgets, then the senator had the right to receive an annual payment on the excess or leave it in the business as a sort of slush fund for rainy days. Mr. Davis always referred to this scenario as "possibilities." The elder man had just stared past him into the azure sky with that twinkle in his eyes when Dan asked him what those "possibilities" might look like.

"Let's just say this ride isn't over for me yet, Dan. My wife says it's keeping me young."

Since the business had experienced a few pleasant surprises with regard to revenues and growth, Dan decided it was unlikely that the likes of Ashley Press and his gang of vultures would be darkening his office doorstep anytime soon. Of course, if Ashley was pushing a shopping cart through the store aisles, Dan figured that type of turnabout was fair play.

Ben interrupted his thoughts, saying, "Dan, it's time you expanded."

"You mean the store?" he stammered. "No way. I just cleared up Father's mess and I can't fund anything out of cash flow. I can tell you that. I just got my mother settled. I tell you, Ben, I've never felt like I had a reasonable amount of money in my life and I'm just starting to like my circumstances. Absolutely not," he stated emphatically with a slap on the desk to ensure Ben understood.

Ben was nothing if not a patient listener, and he let his younger friend gradually run out of steam. "Dan you are what—25, 26? Is this it? You're satisfied? By the way, I don't mean your store here, although I think we should also consider enlarging the footprint of this operation at the same time the new stores are opened." Ben could see that Dan might need some convincing.

"Store...s? What the devil are you talking about? We're doing reasonably well here, Ben, but I'm not prepared to risk it all on some expansion ego trip."

Ben listened and nodded knowingly. "Yes, you're probably right, and what I came to share with you isn't for you. There's probably some other sharp operator in the grocery business out there who wants to seize the moment and take advantage of what our family's real-estate advisors are telling us will be unprecedented population growth in this area of the country in the next 20 to 30 years," Ben teased. "They've modelled this using everything at their disposal and are telling us there will be a bonanza in land valuations and to take advantage of the opportunities in some of the promising urban centers we know of around here now. I came out of a meeting we held last week intrigued to say the least. We like it a lot and feel that the premise is sound enough that we're going to make a significant investment, but we will be bringing in strategic partners." Dan noticed that Ben closed his eyes as he spoke, painting a vista in his mind of all that he described.

"Our premise is to grow these land acquisitions out in those cities and towns that we understand for now and then re-evaluate. This is a game changer for our family, Dan, and something we've done a tremendous amount of due diligence on."

Now really warming to his concept, Ben explained further. "I've been noticing something happening now for several years. I see families moving into the city, coming from areas of the world I frankly haven't ever heard of before but that doesn't make their desire to experience this country any different from our own. Immigration," he explained to Dan," was a story that would prove to be the key to many future fortunes for those who paid attention to it as an opportunity instead of a threat.

"Dan, you are running a fine operation here. My concern is you never seem to lift your head up long enough to acknowledge yourself. Many people in town and in this industry consider you to be a first class operator. Your revenues alone tell the story, and the fact that you've thought to align your supplier relationships with your customers' wants and needs is where I think the future of your business lies.

"What Doug tells me about your staff here makes me think you have a few potential future store managers already, and you can hire those you don't have in place for departmental heads, like the meat shops. Our thought is we need a grocery market in each of our developments. The big established players will want too much from us. We're leery of unequal relationships amongst our tenant operations, so we're looking for those likeminded entrepreneurs we can grow with. I want you in with me on this, Fortune, but I won't ask twice," Ben said.

Dan felt he was well beyond succumbing to the urgency but thought back to Ben's advice of a few years back and how he had been instrumental in hooking him up with Mr. Davis. That Dan knew of no business reason for Ben to help him earlier was why he felt he owed him the benefit of the doubt.

While he always insisted on seeing something in writing, Dan gradually started to tune in to his friend's de facto sales pitch. He listened carefully and thought of what he had achieved to this point. What Ben had said was true. It seemed ridiculous that here he was in his mid-20s and his thoughts were on protecting what he had. At the same time he didn't know if Ben really understood that Dan felt lucky to have anything and that the events surrounding his entry into the family business had been nothing short of traumatizing.

His thoughts drifted to Marnie and their upcoming wedding. Marnie was now out of school and wanting to enter work in her professional field. Was it fair to ask her to give it all up? Their wedding would be in approximately 10 weeks, and Dan felt his level of preparedness was midway between slim and none. He didn't even own a suit.

Turning his mind back to Ben, he let out a big sigh and said, "I am probably not able to be involved but tell me how this all would work."

Hold, Fold or Double Down

Ben pushed the term sheet across the desk toward Dan. As he did, he said, "We'd love to make you part of this, Dan, and you know I think highly of what you've done with the store and all. But this takes you into a whole new level, and it's important that you get a sense of what all this means. Once you decide you want to be involved, that is," he added.

"I had Mr. Gates, the legal mind at our offices, draft this earlier today specifically for our conversation. I knew that my coming forward with this would give you a bit of a jolt, but I want you to pay very close attention as I go through this," Ben said.

Dan read the document and then reread it. It had some interesting elements and to his mind really tied the two businesses at the hip for better or worse. He wondered if he had it in him to take the leap of faith and go down this road with Ben. So many things could go wrong. Multiple locations? At times he felt barely able to handle one. That he, let alone Rebekah and Peter, could be part of a senior management team was not something that had even crossed his mind before today. As he thought of them, he realized he had seen things in both that signified a commitment to the Market that was beyond that of a typical employee who held the job merely as a means to an end.

Dan knew in his heart that he had a special drive to succeed that was extraordinary. He hoped he was a multiplier of others efforts and not a diminisher like his father had been, managing his employees through abject fear and intimidation.

"Ben, I don't have much experience with documents like these, and as you know, my legal career was over before it started. What does all this mean to me?"

"That's a good question," Ben replied. "But before I take you through it, what professionals are you working with these days? I think you should get some legal counsel on this. What we have here is just a term sheet but we will be documenting this in a contract before we get underway."

"If you're asking whether I retain a lawyer, I must admit that through my dealing with Mr. Press here in town I was left with a bad taste in my mouth," he said without much emotion. "If I hadn't done what was necessary, my mother would have been out on the street, and I resent Press for putting her in that position."

Ben's body language showed that he had something to say, but Dan kept talking. "I mistrust the profession, Ben. I know my father put himself in a bind by not responding to the industry and the demands of the business but I can't help feeling that Ashley Press and his crowd took advantage of him."

Now it was Ben's turn to talk. "Dan you might be being unfair to a profession that has all kinds of genuine people in it. You really can't take this business any further unless you extend some trust to others, including outsourced professionals." He continued, knowing that he didn't want their discussion to go off the rails because of Dan's longstanding feelings on the issue. "Now, before I take you through this document, I want you to ask me any questions that may come to mind or ask me for clarification if you're unclear on any of the terminology. So let's cover this now and not get ahead of ourselves before you understand this term sheet."

    a. By Curtis Development Corporation (CDC):

        i. Site selection and building of new store facilities to specifications established by FFM. Development to be on a cost plus basis.

"What this means is as a development company we need from you all the things you know about store layout. You'll need to work with a layout and design company that we work with in order to give your thoughts on what's needed. We want to build sites that work today but with tomorrow in mind. With your input, our intention is to put up stores that reflect modern requirements. They will be spacious facilities—bigger than this place—with delivery docks and direct-to-floor capacity in the back end so that all inventory is for sale right after it arrives. That will improve cash flow right there."

> ii. Provide store facilities to FFM on lease-to-own terms reflective of each local market's conditions.

"This point is probably obvious, but the reason we need your knowledge on design is that you're going to own these outright at some point and so I'm sure you, as much as we, need to get it right. In a development like we're envisioning, I'm sure a few things will evolve out of the first location built that we'll want to adjust, but the fewer of those we have the better. We want a continuity that fits the overall development, and then it will be easy to duplicate in various areas as we grow things out."

> iii. Provide a secured private credit facility:
>
>> 1. Up to [$yyyyy] per location and a maximum aggregate of (3 times $xxxxx)

"This is effectively 'equity financing,' so that you can build other market locations sooner than FFM's cash flow would be able to support," Ben explained. "We're responsible for overall site selection and will identify what goes where and when. Our plan is to get a shovel in the ground right away on some land we acquired some time ago. The one we feel is suitable for our first project sits on the edge of the city, smack dab in the middle of the largest residential development the municipality has ever planned.

"A hospital, schools, parks, playgrounds, an arena, forested green space and let's not forget a state-of-the-art FFM where everyone can get their groceries."

Dan had always admired Ben's ability to explain his ideas, and what he was hearing sent an unexpected shiver down his spine.

Ben continued to relate his vision to the younger man. "Personally, I'm out of the office two to three days a week, identifying locations in the municipalities we will target. I've been to more urban planning meetings than a guy should have to attend in five lifetimes, but I'm learning an awful lot. As we divulge our overall concept, I'm finding we have cities and towns lining up for us. They're excited and know that with the population growth, having the right cross section of amenities, goods and services for these families is going to drive other opportunities."

Yeah, like taxes, Dan imagined, sardonically keeping his pessimistic views on government to himself.

"Now another thing you should be aware of, from our perspective: this provision puts a cap on the amount that our family may be called upon to fund at any one point in time and the amount that we need to keep on standby for this purpose," Ben pointed out.

"Similarly, we need to determine how fast FFM can scale out its management, build teams and put an appropriate work force in place. Your ability to manage through others rather than do things yourself will be critical. I have a lot of faith in you, though, Dan. I was describing you to some of the others at our CDC offices the week before last and your ears must have been burning. I concluded with a statement I truly believe in: 'This guy gets it.' He is what we're looking for, and if we can find some others like him for our other anchors, we have a winner and this will be a great investment.

"In this term sheet I have arbitrarily set this at the estimated cost of three market locations. We already have at least three sites in our land holdings now. The cost per location would have to be developed together and agreed to. From your perspective, this gives you some room to grow FFM at a reasonable rate. This loan would rank behind other traditional creditors, being suppliers and banks, providing working capital." Ben gave a laugh and said, "As developers we have yet to figure out a way to get those traditional creditors to look after us first."

> 2. Carry base annual interest rate of prime plus 1% plus participation in net profits before taxes of 5%

"This is a provision that adds two-way value to the relationship. Obviously we will both have skin in the game throughout this project. However, our profit participation is something that ensures you that we will do everything in our power to make this venture work. Issues will come up on some of these sites that having the landlord involved will be both a time and money saver to FFM. It doesn't make sense for us to be invoicing you for what might be very minor nuisance items. This ensures that our whole organization is wedded to the concept of doing the little things to help each other out. In my experience, interested eyes looking at the small stuff allows the big picture to take care of itself.

"Who knows? When you make your millions, Dan, you may want to pour some of that back into an investment in CDC," Ben said, chuckling.

"Well, we are quite a ways from that being an option." Dan smiled, surprised at himself that he was actually starting to see a future alongside his friend.

> 3. Loan to be secured by all assets of FFM

He was soon brought back to reality when Ben pointed out the securitization being requested. "So if I am not everything you think I am, I could lose not only the new sites but my store here as well?" Dan asked, his heart suddenly finding a new home in his throat. Was it him, he wondered, or did the room's temperature suddenly rise a few degrees?

"Yep," said Ben letting the answer hang in the air without defining it in any way. He paused for more than a few moments and then stated what he considered the crux of entrepreneurship: "Dan, you don't win big if you don't make big gambles. I believe you will find in both your professional and personal lives that there will be no way to sail with one foot planted on shore. Your security is within you, Dan, not in anyone else. You of all people should understand that with what you've done in the last four years.

"The young lady you're marrying—tell me, do you love her?" Ben prodded. Dan rapidly nodded his acknowledgement. "Did you ask her for a guarantee? Did you ask her for three letters of reference from other fellows she's dated that say she's an upfront and honest person? The nature of our relationships, Dan—the ones that really last and have value to both parties—is based on trust. Of course we're both going to need to put this in a form of contract, but I believe that looking into each other's eyes is a good way to know how things will eventually work out. If I thought this was in question we wouldn't be having this conversation."

> 4. Debt convertible to equity in FFM at the discretion of CDC on the following terms

"I did ask Mr. Gates to include the provision marked 4, though, to give both sides some latitude and protection. As indicated above, the proposed financing is essentially equity in nature but by making it 'convertible debt' and deferring the conversion to a future date, this allows you to prove yourself," Ben explained.

> a. In the event of default at any time after date of first draw down—total debt including outstanding base interest cost at date of notice of intention to convert/estimated FMV of FFM at that time.

Ben furthered his point by stating his own perspective. The secured debt with a fixed and preferred rate of return gave his family some security against the chance of Dan's potential failure. "As you see, we would preserve a minimum conversion rate in the event of success under (b) (i) below. Dan, if you were to default as contemplated in 4 (a), we wouldn't likely convert but rather would exercise our security against assets of FFM, unless we felt we could turn it around and wanted the equity to potentially take control of the locations on a going concern basis. My guess is, though, that you're a good operator and we won't be doing that.

"On the other hand, 4 (b)(ii) permits you to reduce the level of dilution from the base set out in 4(b)(i), that is if FFM can provide a return that exceeds the minimum target rate of return on the convertible debt."

> b. In the event of no default any time after 3 years from date of first draw down
>
>> i. (total debt including outstanding base interest cost at date of notice of intention to convert/estimated FMV of FFM) x 100%;
>>
>> ii. Conversion rate set out in (i) above reduces at the rate of 10% for every 1% actual annualized rate of return in excess of the base interest rate earned by CDC and paid by FFM up to the date of notice of intention to convert;

Dan listened to Ben and found himself once again relaxing a bit and able to think about what he was hearing and ponder its potential. He would not be making up his mind today. It just wasn't in his nature to jump at things without measured thought, but it appeared to him that Ben and CDC's window for him was not going to be a large one. He asked Ben to continue with the document and clarify his expectations of FFM.

> b. By FFM
>
>> i. Enter into lease-to-own agreements for all new grocery stores developed by CDC within specified area and timeframe

"Dan, you haven't yet had access to all the data that we've seen from the study we contracted," said Ben, slowing his words down for maximum impact. "I have read it inside, outside and backward. I believe it is sound thinking and correct in its assumptions on future growth and the demographic that will drive that growth. I can add that this strategy, once embarked upon, is a defining risk for my stewardship of CDC and our family holdings. I can't say I'm never wrong but my track record of being right when it really counts is one I would put up against anyone's."

> ii. Agreement to operate FFM on locations for terms of lease and to maintain specified quality standards

"As I said earlier, we have no doubt you are a strong operator and, just looking around, it's impressive how you keep this store in what I can tell you is an outdated facility. I know that moving your act into better sites is going to be a good move. I have complete faith in you on that point."

Dan grimaced as Ben spoke of his building. It had been in the family for 45 years. Double F had acquired it in some way that wasn't necessarily above board, but he had gone into business just the same and withstood the Great Depression, which had no doubt shaped him and his business practices through outright fear as much as anything else.

> iii. Exclusivity to leasing from CDC within specified region

Dan couldn't see that this part would be a problem, as he didn't know anyone else with grandiose dreams like Ben's.

> iv. CDC to have seat on board of directors of FFM

Dan had never imagined that he would be involved in an enterprise requiring a board of directors. He usually liked to run his own show and have total control of what he was involved in. He could see himself struggling with this last point.

On this point he was right. Dan Fortune would struggle with control issues for some time to come, both at FFM and in his personal life.

He walked Ben to the main doors of the now deserted market, absent-mindedly reaching up to face a few cans of coffee to the front so the shelves looked full, as they walked to the front end. They shook hands at the door.

"Well, I'm going to need a few days," Dan said. "But I want to thank you for giving me this opportunity. I am just not sure."

Ben Curtis smiled as he left the Market and strolled away, hearing Dan turning the lock behind him over his shoulder. Pragmatic enough to maintain focus on his own plan regardless of Dan's involvement, he still inwardly pulled for his young friend to make the right move and join the Curtis Development Corp. in this new venture. He always felt he was a good judge of character and knew that, if he found enough others with the type of commitment Dan had for his business, a bright future for everyone involved was inevitable. Accumulating a solid core of other like-minded independent business people was the center of Ben's master concept.

His mind drifted to what he found was an increasingly easy mental picture to form: a shopping development that provided an answer to one of those essential requirements for modern families and what they would grow to depend on—convenient hours, free parking, wide open common spaces and a fetching array of products and services all under one massive roof.

He reasoned that just about anyone could put up a building. Once that was in place, the products could be brought in and initial customers would take care of themselves. The big value creator, he decided, would be in assembling a group of forward-thinking business people. They all needed to be in for the long haul. The very act of proximity to one another would add value to each other's businesses, not unlike the formation of the great commercial settlements in an earlier century.

Over the next few years, it would be hard work and long hours. There wouldn't be a lot of time for outside pursuits, but Ben understood himself well. He had always known that in working hard, one had to find some sort of balance within one's lifestyle; important pillars of life like family and health had to be embraced alongside the pursuit of success. Others in his own family had made it clear to Ben that achieving superior results was gratifying. However, the journey in getting to one's ultimate destination could also be a tremendous gauge of what life was really about for those with entrepreneurial mindsets.

Lost in thought, Ben became aware that it was starting to rain, just lightly. There was an ominous look to the darkening sky. Across the nearby hills, dull rolling thunder and a few flickers of distant lightening pulled what was left of the diminished daylight toward it. The rain intensified and Ben welcomed its refreshment.

He had always thought that the way an overnight rainfall cleansed a town's streets and sidewalks presented a freshened palette of possibility to anyone in touch with life's true potential. He paused at his car and turned the key to pop the trunk so he could get out his umbrella.

Were there other entrepreneurs out there in similar situations to Fortune's who were also running good operations? Could they complement CDC and be as good a fit as Dan?

"Of course there are," Ben said aloud to no one in particular. The streets were full of people hustling to get out of the storm, and no one was paying any attention to him. His umbrella overhead, he ambled down the main street where he was meeting Ginny, her parents and the kids for a late dinner, whistling as he went.

Part II

Salad Days

"Where are those store reports I've been asking for? I've been off the phone for five minutes now, and I need them. Come on, move it, ladies, make it happen—today—now!" Fanny Farver Fortune wasn't having a great day, and her frustration mounted as she yelled through her open doorway into the hall. Her two assistants definitely knew when she was reaching her boiling point and were, as always, overreacting to her temper. They were ineffectively running around in tandem in the outer office, trying to change the toner cartridge in the printer and accommodate the request. At the same time, they both studiously avoided eye contact with the scion of the Fortune family, Fanny. She was the eldest of Dan and Marnie's four children and had worked in the family firm for over a decade.

Fanny was not one to suffer others' mistakes with grace or those that she considered not as hardworking or bright as she was. It was best the assistants decided to endure her outbursts, as they felt strangely deserving but didn't understand why. They both figured they wouldn't be around long anyway. Fanny in her role as the company's director of customer experience had historically gone through assistants at a much higher turnover rate than the rest of the senior management team of Fortune Consolidated Industries combined.

Fanny's father, Dan, knew all about her working style and her lack of tact and intellectual humility when working with others. He knew that Fanny thought she was being just like her father, but tried too hard and often diminished her co-workers in order to finish something as fast as possible. He also knew of his eldest's predisposition to treat employees as a disposable commodity, not understanding the immense costs to FCI of the chronic cycle of hiring, training, firing and rehiring. He wondered why she considered this acceptable practice when he himself had always placed a high value on family loyalty and team in his own approach to business.

When Fanny was just a child, her father had let slip one day in a conversation with his brother Peter that he saw a lot of their own father in her. Even as a child she had exhibited an aggressive nature that was similar to his father's. Peter could see it as well, and together they had laughingly branded her "Triple F."

The cascading success of his food industry-related businesses built up through the years had softened Dan's recall on Double F and the iron grip of intimidation he had exerted on his employees. The company had grown. FCI was and continued to be privately held by Dan Fortune and a family trust. He had complete control, considering himself rather like a benevolent despot. He was kindly, but demanded strict adherence to a winning set of principles that he understood and lived by but couldn't quite easily articulate if asked to speak to the reasons for his success.

Dan was a wealthy man. As he pointed out to his family, the name *Fortune* was on every FCI building they owned in some form or another. At last count, 75 retail stores blanketed every population center of any note in the central part of the country. A wholly owned food wholesaling distribution subsidiary, FCI Foods produced, packaged and delivered foods to FCI stores as well as other smaller chains.

FCI Foods included the combined output of a fresh and processed meat operation, fresh produce company, frozen foods division, dairy and several other divisions that represented much of what appeared on the shelves of most FCI locations. By controlling the supply chain, Dan felt FCI was unassailable by most of the traditional competitive factors other stores faced.

In his fifties, his ownership of a vast piece of the necessary supply chain network had come out of the blue when his old friend Pudge had phoned FCI's corporate offices looking to set up a meeting. Puzzled at the formality, he buzzed RJ on the intercom and asked her what this could be about. She replied that her brother would be approaching him to gauge his interest in buying out a controlling interest in his meat processing business. Over the years, Dan had relied on Pudge's company to exclusively supply FCI stores with what became more than 80% of the store's fresh meat.

Pudge's business had grown in lockstep with Dan's as FCI had evolved in its relationship with CDC's properties as the anchor tenant for new developments. Unfortunately, Pudge had developed a heart condition. It wasn't critical, but as he said when he came to Dan, his parents had worked themselves to early graves and if giving up a large chunk of his business would remove a lot of the stress, why not?

He could stay involved at the level he wanted to but still enjoy life as much as he could and look after his health. Pudge explained, "Dan, I am 54 years old and the doctor said if I don't change my ways he can't guarantee me anything." He went on edging toward the point of his visit. "Our relationship has allowed me to be about a hundred times more than I ever thought I could be in life and, dammit, I am going to enjoy myself. That business, though, those stockyards, plants and what has been created from my end are going to fetch a good price on the open market, but I wanted to come to you first. I owe you that and I know RJ would never speak to me again if I went outside our relationship."

"Not sure what I can do, Pudge, but I'll move on this one way or another soon. Thank you for bringing this matter to me. I will miss dealing with you business-to-business, but having you as a friend upright and breathing is more important. Give me three weeks and I'll come back and either launch a bid or step away. Is that fair?"

Ben Curtis had been a godsend to Dan, a straight shooter in their professional relationship and a helluva friend to Dan on a personal level. Their conversations always picked up where they left off, and Dan considered Ben's judgment on most matters beyond reproach. It took a phone call with Ben and a round or two of golf and Dan had made up his mind to get into the meat business. Several more times over the years in seemingly never-ending cycles, FCI was built by acquisition, piece by piece.

This included the fresh produce division that quickly morphed into fresh and frozen as the capacity to do that had evolved. The produce piece was something Dan considered a crown jewel in his empire, and he smiled when he thought of its genesis coming out of that unlikely starting point of two young teens who had only each other and a baby on the way. He recalled Beth walking home from school with him and giving him her unique perspectives on life while he absorbed everything.

She and her husband had taken what he knew—which was agriculture—and with her drive, moved from roadside stands to their involvement with the Fortune Family Market as a supplier. They innovated, failed, and innovated again, eventually finding the formula that worked. A simple farming operation had evolved into processing and packaging. The couple had now forged a tremendous business, supplying not only FCI, but other chains as well. In the last years they had acquired controlling interest in a California distribution business, which allowed them to scale out with advanced fresh product logistics technology.

In the end, Beth and her husband Bob's marriage was a happy union and, as the children they'd had early in life grew up and moved away, the couple became more involved in their church. They started to nurture a deep interest in service to others less fortunate.

Beth had never mentioned anything to Dan, but he knew her own experience as a teenage mother had left an indelible mark on her. Teaching others about family planning was important to her. She knew that the story she and Bob had written in blood, sweat and tears was certainly one of hard work. However, she was also aware that the capacity for hard work didn't always end up in the level of financial success they'd been blessed with. In their case, she was a believer in providence.

At what they considered to be an appropriate juncture, they let Dan know that they were planning a complete divesture of their business so that they could move to a Caribbean island as missionaries. Life was hard there, and things we take for granted here like fresh water, health care and youth education were scarce. The island had suffered a devastating earthquake in the previous year, and the couple had decided this was where they needed to be. In the end, Dan was their buyer and Beth and Bob Allan went to pursue their purpose.

Dan had even found a way to involve his father in the business as it existed today. A small start-up firm had come to him with a concept product, a line of premium salad dressings. They wanted a place on the shelves at his stores. After trying the product at the Fortune household, and getting positive feedback from friends and family on its taste, he hatched a plan.

He made sure the salad dressing was field tested in his stores with free samples, and again the reports were positive. Then he went back to the fledgling company and said he would indeed give them shelf space, but wanted to brand the line himself in exchange for seed capital and controlling interest in their firm.

With a faraway look in his eyes he said, "I think I would like to call our salad dressing line, 'Old Grocer.' The type font will be Antique and we'll put a lithograph print of a caricature of an old grocer on the label. And who knows? We may go further into other product lines. And …" He paused and went on, "I have just the face to put on that label." He opened the top right-hand drawer of his desk and pulled out an aged photograph of Double F.

"Gentlemen, I have very few pictures of my father. This is the one and only picture I have of him where he is smiling." He carefully laid the old photo on his desktop pad. "Should you agree to my conditions, we have a deal and we can start moving this line into all our stores."

They shook hands and Dan's salad days were truly in high gear.

The Next-Generation Women

While he was growing up as the son of Double F, life was so unpleasant that Dan's principle objective was to get out of town and not be subjected to any abuse himself. But, as the song said, life was what happened when you were busy making other plans. All the employees from that era had long since passed on. Now that they were a few years into their 70s, Dan and Peter were really the only ones left from the pre-FCI Fortune Family Market days who remembered Double F, but Fanny let him know by her approach to work that Fletcher Fortune had a legacy.

Fanny was married and had two children of her own, with husband Al Strong. They had met early on and had kind of hung on to each other for around a decade before deciding that both could commit to marriage. So they started their family a little later than most parents of their children's friends.

Al raised quarter horses on a hobby farm that was attached to the estate property where they lived north of the city. The area had been wholly gentrified over the previous two or three decades by a huge influx of wealth. The financial windfalls allowed those with the means to purchase picturesque properties and turn them into dream worlds. Opulent, carefully detailed and well-kept farms contradicted the ingrained rural values of those who had hacked this farmland from the original woodlands that blanketed its rolling hills and early settlements.

One of their neighbors had even made a name for herself internationally, starting with a homemaking television show that espoused good living and was now a brand all her own. For Al, the irony was that she was selling a conceptual idea that bridged the gap between how things once were to how people with the economic means could live today. No one in the area saw her much, but that was typical of many of them, Al thought, who considered themselves country squires. Al often thought that the people whose lives and pictures were profiled at the local museum would have been amazed at the changes, and he wasn't necessarily certain that the changes were positive.

For his part, Al kept his head down, funded worthy causes like the museum, and tried to do what he felt would make him happy. Fanny worried him a bit as she was so wrapped up in FCI that he felt the need to be both father and mother to Danny and Samantha. His relationship with his spouse was played out on her terms. His role was to be there for her, be there for the children and be there for her family, in that order.

Originally from the west, Al had first connected with Fanny through friends on a ski trip. Fanny's style of skiing was to lead the pack and decide the routes down the mountain for all of them. He saw her as a take charge person. She had so much energy that most people gave her control and once given it wasn't easily relinquished. Al had found her style quite attractive then, but it had grown to wear him down over the years to the point that he consciously backed down if he thought conflict with her was in the air.

His friends teasingly referred to him as Mr. Fanny Fortune, saying they wished they could have his life as a kept man. Al grimaced at the thought and said nothing, but it bothered him when he focused on it. He didn't have anyone to talk with about his feelings and had engaged more than one therapist over the years so he could verbalize how he felt.

He had explained to each one that he knew he loved Fanny, and had known what she was like long before they had married, but at times he didn't like her. Each therapist would listen and empathize, or at least appear to, but not provide any tangible directions. That is, other than suggesting that he and Fanny come in together. Al would feel good about things until he jumped into his truck in the parking lot, thought about asking his wife to attend and realized he didn't need the argument.

His next booking always disappeared off the therapist's appointment log in due course, once he took care of his bill. He would eventually engage someone new in the profession when the relationship troubled him more than usual, and the circle would begin anew. He didn't get a lot of joy out of the status of being a wealthy couple and the high profile functions they attended. Instead, his real joy was his horses and being among them, working day to day, mucking stalls and stepping in where needed with the trainers, grooms and stable hands. He was much more hands-on than the gentleman farmer that Fanny seemed to wish he was.

Inge Petterson stood in the back of the foyer, which was far from a simple entry hall to a building. Fortune Hall, as it was moments away from being christened, was where a large crowd of the area's movers and shakers had gathered to see and be seen. At this point in the program, several community benefactors were being acknowledged for making contributions to the various exhibit areas that were part of the city's long-awaited Gallery of Modern Art. It was a truly gorgeous afternoon and sunlight was streaming in through large windows that, on first glance, didn't appear to be held up by anything except the other massive panes of glass.

If you looked up at the architecture, you could feel the tug of the blue sky in the wide open space of the building. Inge felt it pull her spirit so that it soared, seeking to reflect the intended design concept of mankind's continuing collective imagination. The design was a tribute to the renaissance lineage of Michelangelo, da Vinci and right back to the early origins of man and those that chronicled human development in the art forms of that age and existence. It was space that a common builder would have thought a waste—there was room enough for several more floors—but that was not how truly great architects like the renowned Mr. Luis Fernando de Sousa thought. Inge had five years ago traveled to Sao Paolo, Brazil, to meet Nando—the great man—and lure him back to create the building they were celebrating that day.

And lure him she did, with every possible angle at her disposal. He'd been a joy to know and she felt happy about their relationship even though it had now come to an end. Nando wasn't here to see the unveiling as he had found himself immersed in other projects elsewhere on the globe and had left her and his beautiful creation behind.

Inge became considerably more tense of body, mind and tongue as she knew that the opening ceremony was building to a climax and she was expected to get to the dais and make a speech to the crowd. It was easier, she had decided, to give a talk to discerning fellow collectors and enthusiasts, as they understood her and were much more part of her world. Her group of activists and friends had those critical special interests at heart and knew that if they didn't push their ideas and values about the arts, this point of view could easily get lost in today's "every man for himself" (or woman for herself) mentality. Early in her adult life she had decided that her life would be different and that she felt more a part of her world with this passion for aesthetic creativity.

She bristled at the thought of her sister Fanny's influence on civic, regional and national politicians of all stripes just because of who she was and the family business. Little did all her sister's hangers-on realize that their father was the master puppeteer and those strings were long indeed. No, she acknowledged, her father was not giving any signs yet that he felt like ceding control to anyone. She knew he wanted the best for everybody but couldn't understand why she and her siblings weren't all behind each other and stronger in their solidarity to take FCI into what he felt was a bright future.

She knew her father's health struggles had awakened in him a sense of purpose around what he and their mother would eventually leave behind. He didn't—or more correctly, couldn't—understand the dynamics of their family and how everyone was coming at things from different angles and viewpoints. Why couldn't they embrace the status quo and be appreciative of their place in the world? He would often remind them all that the Fortunes came from modest beginnings and that there was not enough of the old home town left in any of them.

Now in front of the crowd at the dedication ceremony, all would acknowledge Inge was a striking woman, tall with long, naturally blond hair, and blessed with the piercing ice blue eyes from the Nordic forbears on her mother's side. Intimidating to most men on her appearance alone, her goal was not necessarily a comfortable long-term relationship. She told herself she was a continuation of the great traditions of the upper end of society: a divorcée who wasn't going to give in again to a man who didn't share her unique views and love of beautiful things. She certainly didn't need a man for financial support, as she often reminded herself.

Her experiences in a short-lived marriage to Alfie, a Norwegian man she'd met while traveling in Europe, had in the end decided this point of view. She learned that her ex-husband had been deceitful and more in love with the Fortune money, and its capacity to fund his bobsledding dreams, than really wanting to create anything with her. However, that seemed like a long time ago and, on the near side of forty, she was fixed on her own vision; a static relationship was not something she really aspired to. Eventually, Alfie was confronted by some rather obvious evidence of wrongdoing involving performance-enhancing drugs, and he was stripped of his right to compete for two years.

Dan Fortune had supported the team for a couple of seasons at this point and always wished he could get to an event somewhere but other obligations always got in the way. He was dismayed to hear about the banishment. Worse, though, was that he learned from a contact inside the team that his son-in-law was being a bit too much of a player on the Bobsleigh Grand Prix circuit; he'd neglected to mention to some of the ladies that regularly followed the circuit that he was married.

Inge bit her upper lip when she recalled how Alfie had been invited to a private meeting with Inge's father, where he was quietly paid to vacate the premises. The amount would keep him in bobsleds, fur coats, fine champagne and all the female admirers he could handle for a long time to come. The other members of the family were aware of what had happened, the amount and the end result and chose to move on. It certainly rankled some to think of paying off such a large amount to someone they had identified as an obvious cad from the start.

With mixed feelings about philanthropy, she wished her family would just allow her to give freely with no strings attached to causes that she deemed worthy. Events like these seemed like a lot of backslapping and self-congratulations. Did it add anything to the experience of art appreciation? She thought not and waited as the head of the foundation started into his long introduction of the gallery's lead funder.

Looking around at the grand space and lost in her thoughts, she pondered what it all meant to those who were gathered. After all, wasn't the purpose to expose others to the same joys that art brought out in her? Her valuing of altruistic pursuits and social causes that served others was topped only by her preferences for all things aesthetic. Seeing form, harmony and beauty in both nature and that which was wrought by man was her central passion. Not that she felt much of a kinship with the genius she saw in others. Besides, viewing, experiencing, listening to and evaluating what was formed by the hands, hearts and minds of people she admired was her life's focus.

She heard the introduction ending and slowly made her way to the steps of the dais atop of which the director curator stood applauding her. The crowd parted, making way as she came through the room. She smiled and acknowledged many that she knew, shaking hands, not giving away how vulnerable she felt. Rising up the steps, she accepted warm embraces from both the DC and the foundation head, who'd been tasked with introducing her.

She moved quickly into her prepared comments, hoping the audience couldn't sense her nerves. She soon rounded into form and turned her talk away from the family donation and toward her views on what having a suitable showcase for exhibits could mean to the area. She was just about to move into some of the student internships and educational programs when she noticed a loud commotion on the edge of the room by one of the main sculpture exhibits.

More of the crowd took their focus off of her and on to what was happening, and she audibly gasped into the microphone as she noticed who was at the center of the to-do. A younger man was trying to shake off one of the catering staff who had restrained him after another had refused him an additional glass of wine.

"Let me go, you idiots. I own—" His protests drifted away as he was quickly ushered from the main space down a side hall out of listening range. It was apparent to all that the man had been over-served, and everyone there looked sideways at each other in the uncomfortable silence that followed.

Turning their attention back to the dais, Inge smiled weakly and carried on, rapidly moving into her concluding statements. Not acknowledging the warm congratulations of those with her on the dais, she quickly stepped down and slipped out the side door as the string quartet started and the afternoon's proceedings continued. She banged through the exit, seething in her embarrassment. Acknowledging no one in the outer walkways, Inge fled to the parking lot.

Waiting beside her car was the young fellow that had caused the disruption.

"Sorry, Sis," her obviously intoxicated brother whimpered.

The Bust

Inge thought about just jumping into her coupe and driving away, leaving her brother Jimmy to find his own way home, but assessed the potential damage should Jimmy get behind the wheel and thought better of that option. "Get in the car, Jimmy," she commanded. Docile as always when he knew he was in trouble, her brother got into the passenger side and tried to explain his way out of trouble.

"That bastard almost broke my arm, Sis," Jimmy led off. "I told him I just wanted another drink and he told me I was cut off. I only had two glasses of wine. Weren't we paying for all of it? I swear some of the stuck-up snobs around here don't realize how a place like that ever got built."

"Shut up, I don't want to hear it. You have a serious problem and all this needs to stop. That's the last straw, Jimmy," Inge said in a quiet but determined voice. "You're a mess and obviously arrived drunk to begin with. How did you get there? Why did you come?"

"Lefty dropped me off. We were just shooting some pool, havin' a few pops, you know," he slurred.

"No, I don't know, Jimmy. I don't know what it's like to drink all afternoon with your loser friends and think that somehow that's a productive day. Do you realize how many people there would know you, at least by our family name anyway? When Mom and Dad hear about this it's going to really hurt them. They … we all … had so much hope that the valley retreat you went to could fix you and get you back to where we all know you can be. I tell you, Jimmy, you're out of chances. If this is how you wish to live your life so be it, but no one will support you. Come on—make something of yourself."

"Like you did?" said Jimmy after a long pause. He looked out the side window, not wanting her to see the tears streaming down his face.

"Like I did? What the hell do you mean by that?"

Jimmy was the youngest Fortune and had arrived quite a while after the other three. Twelve years in fact. His birth had signalled the end of an unlikely crisis for Dan and Marnie. Dan was away from his family quite a lot in those years and hadn't understood that the ties that bind were fraying within the family. He was a provider, and sometimes providers forget life's critical balance. "Are we living to work or working to live, Dan?" his wife would cajole.

"Marnie, I am doing this for all of you. Let's get away to the cottage, just you and me. Soon." He would try to soothe her with promises like these that never seemed to come to fruition.

"Why can't we be like Ben and Ginny were?" she would scold.

Before Ginny passed away, she told Marnie that she felt she'd done what was necessary to get her family to a point where they could all experience what it felt like to be self-reliant. "They have all they want and more. We've raised some great young adults that have found careers, even two of them working in the business."

With the business clearly rolling and under full sail by the time Jimmy arrived, the youngest of the family couldn't identify with the ups and downs of what it took to build FCI. When he asked for something, he quickly got it from a somewhat guilty father, often against Marnie's wishes. The conflict in their parenting values continued, but always below the surface and unnoticeable except to those who were personally connected to the family.

The management training program Dan had envisioned for FCI had finally become a reality under RJ's leadership. He'd always told his wife that he would be trying to get out more for golf and perhaps even take up flying as he became comfortable with how his burgeoning empire was running.

The stores were good, as were the subsidiary businesses that started as supply offshoots for the retail side but now were self-contained supply chains encompassing most anything involved with food and food service. Dan was at the point where work was a place to go as well as something he felt needed his oversight and direction. But financially he felt no real personal dependency on his paycheck.

Inge guided the car down through the inner city toward where her brother lived. Jimmy had drifted off in the passenger's seat, with his day's activities having now taken their toll on his consciousness. Sobriety would not be within his reach now until the morning.

How could Mom and Dad let him live in such a dump, she thought as they rolled into the main entrance of her brother's condo. They'd felt it was time for Jimmy to grow up and that it wasn't going to happen in the house he'd been raised in with all its amenities and ease of living. Her mother reasoned that giving Jimmy a place he'd have to maintain himself would allow him to grow up. Inge knew that, far from helping him grow up, it was a hangout for his friends who leeched off his money and good nature in return for the sense of belonging they bestowed on him.

She found it strange reasoning on her parent's part that funding a place to stay and ensuring there was money to spend on what she knew was troubling and wrong could somehow be the right way to handle him. Inge knew both her parents loved Jimmy but she could see him slipping away from all of them and into the clutches of a lifestyle her parents couldn't imagine. She had no doubt that, while he didn't admit it, there was more going on in her brother's life than just playing pool and having a few beers.

She herself had had a brush with recreational drug use in her time with Alfie and, while she did partake, she started to notice a change in many of the people in their circle and resolved to step away from it ahead of the breakdown of her marriage.

Going totally natural during the year of the payout to her husband was key to getting back to who she really was. Though it was more emotionally and physically draining than she could have imagined, she was able to cleanse herself of what she thought she wanted, to retreat into the art world where her true calling lay.

The Fortune family had very little understanding or experience with substance abuse at Jimmy's level. In three generations, Double F's austere existence and sober perspective on life had eroded into the chaos that Jimmy had become. She was certain that his ability to play his parents off of one another, her father's guilt and her mother's protective nature, led to an astonishing amount of money going to her brother, well beyond either parent's intention.

She circled into the laneway to the building's entry under the lobby carport. At this time of day, in the waning light, she felt secure as the noise of the city entertainment district was only a block away. The lot itself was well lit and she felt reasonably safe, but she also felt that just on the edge of the darkness there was a street world that Jimmy knew and that knew about Jimmy. It was there, she knew, in the shadows just out of sight. She could feel they were being observed as she reached across to undo his seatbelt and then crossed around the front of the car to open the door for him.

Jimmy came to with a start and, after realizing where he was and how he'd got there, shrugged away his sister's assistance. "I'm okay, Sis. You go on home. Nobody needs to worry about Jimmy." He pitched himself forward and was on his feet, stiffly headed toward the foyer.

The tower was 20 stories high, but, afraid of heights, Jimmy had chosen a place on the ground floor. At least he wouldn't be going up and down the elevator, she decided after she couldn't catch the latch before the door swung closed. She watched through the glass door as far as her line of vision allowed, as he negotiated his way through the building's foyer and then lurched down the hall.

She got back into her idling car, desperate to speak with someone who could help her make sense of the day and the terrible route it had taken to its conclusion. Directing her vehicle into the traffic, she didn't look in her rear-view mirror. If she had, she would have seen one, then two furtive figures emerge from the city blight and move toward the building. They bypassed the entry doors and went directly to the sliding doors a few units down to the east.

Farther away, well on the way back to the expressway by then, Inge would also have seen the two people persistently knocking on her brother's door—louder and louder raps until a light popped on inside and one of the two held a crystalline sac up to the window. They were granted access from within.

There were also others watching all of this unfold, very interested indeed. No one had noticed a rather nondescript car sitting with its engine off in the lot, with two occupants. They'd watched the pretty blond woman get out of her late model luxury car and the unfolding tableau where she helped the person in the passenger side who struggled to get out.

They watched with interest as her occupant had unsteadily got to his feet and then, gaining his bearings and balance, got to the foyer door before shutting it in front of the blonde. They watched her get back to the car and put it into gear.

"Would you do that to her, Sam?" one said to the other after watching her drive away.

"Not a chance; she's a looker," his partner said. Then he whistled as he raised his binoculars back to the sliding doors. "What do you make of our friends' visit?"

"Well, tonight's the night, isn't it. You heard the chief on the news. Let's move."

He reached down, and the undercover vehicle's in-car communications equipment sprang to life. Picking up the handset and speaking deliberately, he said, "OK, Blue Team. All units, it's time to take out the trash and we have some in Remington Heights this evening. We're going to need some coverage on the exits, but let's keep this neat and clean. It looks like there are only three. No need to turn this into anything major."

Big Brother

Inge's hand shook as she pressed the call screen in the coupe, her Bluetooth cellular phone already engaged. Eyes on the road, she knew just where to find the number she was seeking on the top of the right column. The phone engaged and continued to ring 9 to 10 times.

"Oh, c'mon, Jeff, its only 9:30," she sobbed, grimacing through her tears. She and her brother Jeff were only 10-1/2 months apart—so close that with him being a January baby and her born in late November they shared the same birth year and thus went through school in the same grade.

She knew her mother had loved the idea of the two of them being schoolmates. For Inge, being constantly watched over by stable, boring Jeff was something she never thought she'd like, but when he wasn't there for her she felt like a security blanket had been ripped from her grasp. She always had a glimmer of fear that someday he wouldn't be willing or able to help her.

Time and time again it had proven to be an unfounded fear and after a few more rings the phone was picked up and Jeff's deep, reassuring voice came on the line. "Ing, I'm so happy you called. What's up?" Inge could hear a child in the background. "Hang on a minute, Ing," Jeff asked.

"Danni, will you come and get Benjamin?" She could hear him on the phone giving his eldest some brief instruction. "No, you can do it, Danni. You're great at helping out. I'm on the phone with your Auntie Inge." Turning his attention back to her, he explained. "I just gave the kids a bath and was going in to tell them a story. Jennifer's away getting the ski chalet ready for this year and has her sisters up there. They're going to stay up there a few days. The phone rang and I was going to let it go to messages, but I saw it was you. I thought, there are very few people I'm going to pick up for and you are definitely on the list. We're so busy right now at work, but I've been thinking about you the last few days. I've been meaning to check in and see what you're up to."

Inge smiled in relief, finding it easy to imagine him in a domestic role, helping with the children and not needing any outside assistance such as a nanny to make sure the end of the day was taken care of for his brood.

She felt her own maternal instinct had never really developed, but she could enjoy the children of others. As long as they were clean, polite and liked to go to museums. "How are the kids, Jeff?" she asked, losing herself momentarily in her vision of Jeff's family and the joy he took in all five of his children. They ranged in age from 14 months to eight years old, and he and Jennifer were very busy with their upbringing.

When he mentioned Jennifer, Inge's mind drifted to her sister-in-law. If there was one person who even slightly intimidated Inge it was Jennifer. Inge didn't think she had ever come across anyone like Jennifer: poised, beautiful and intelligent along with being a great wife and mother—that was Jennifer. She was the whole package, and what she brought out in Jeff was a sense of purpose and confidence that had eluded him in his youth. He had always been uncomfortable trying to be his father's son.

Jennifer hadn't come into the family as an unknown. She was the adopted and youngest daughter of Ben and Ginny Curtis. By the time of the marriage, the Curtises and the Fortunes had been working in lockstep in the development world for quite a few years, and both generations of both families knew each other well. The Curtises were past what they considered their family-raising years when tragedy had struck their family. Ginny's niece and her husband had been killed in a single car collision late one night. The police report came back inconclusive on the cause, but their two-year-old little girl, Jennifer, was found in the back seat sleeping and unscathed by the carnage.

Ginny quietly approached Ben a few days after the funerals to ask him whether they could as a couple provide a scholarship for Jennifer so that she received the education her parents would have wanted her to have. He asked her for time to give it some thought.

Ben came home a little earlier than usual from his office that day. He went to the fridge and grabbed a drink, and then turned to his wife. "I've been throwing around what you said about doing something for Jennifer and want to thank you for thinking of it. Gin, you really got my mind going, and I believe we need to take that support further and bring Jennifer into our lives. What do you think about us applying to the family court to legally adopt Jennifer? The kids are mostly away at school at this stage, and I think we still have enough energy and love left to raise one more. What do you say?"

Ginny, pondering for a minute, said, "You know I wanted to ask you about that, but wondered if our own children would accept the situation at this point in all of our lives. I know I would love to do it myself. She will eventually probably wonder why her mom is older than the other moms, but ..."

"Ginny you will more than keep up to any of the moms," Ben said gently. "We can do this. We can't think like that. This little girl needs more than our money. She needs our love. The same love we gave all the rest of our children." And that's how Jennifer Curtis became known to Jeff Fortune.

Inge's mind was swept back to the reason for her call. "They are all growing like weeds, Ing," he said. "Danielle came home the other day and said she wanted to be enrolled in afterschool sewing lessons! Can you imagine? Eight years old and coming up with that one? But we called around and she's in with Mrs. Larmer not far from the house. She tells me she'll make me a pair of pants for work. Is that cute or what? And Ollie is way ahead in math and we've been reviewing multiplication tables and I can't stump him! He hasn't even turned seven yet."

Listening, she was always amazed at the animated radiance of Jeff's voice when he spoke of his family and Inge replied, "Sounds like he's a chip off the old block, Jeff."

"Oh I don't know about that, Sis. This kid is really brilliant."

"Well, so were you," she said. "You were always the brightest guy in our class, Jeff, and don't deny it."

Jeff had nurtured a keen interest in learning, which served him well because he seemed to be interested in just about everything. Widely read, he developed a working familiarity with a spectrum of subjects. The pursuit of knowledge and the understanding of truth on things that inspired him were major motivators for her older brother.

She had always felt that he had enough intellectual horsepower for four or five people, but was also gifted with the energy to be cross-functional and excel in any academic discipline he was motivated by. Consequently, Jeff's education had involved a mechanical engineering degree, which was later complemented with a masters in knowledge integration. He had made sure to round out his schooling by taking any electives he could in psychology and human dynamics. Jeff felt most at home leading or contributing to thinking through a problem or puzzle, at work or on the home front.

All he ever wanted in life was to have a career working alongside his father at FCI. Jeff had started at the Markets right at the bottom. At 14, he took any job he was given, mopping floors and packing shoppers' purchases and then later helping keep the strict hygiene of the meat shop with its daily disassembly and reassembly of meat processing equipment. Those present noted that he was extremely adept at mechanical equipment.

Much like his father, he was curious about everything, but mostly about people and things. The diligence with which he applied himself to every project was noted by those he worked around. In the chain he worked in, the nonmanagement staff in each store admired him for these qualities. Although he could have just asked for spending money, instead, he funded himself through his university years. He took various roles at FCI in the cities where he went to school.

Often mocking himself about those jobs, he would make the rest of the family break into gales of laughter. He'd tell stories about going out in the dead of winter and gathering the shopping carts covered in ice and snow through an unplowed parking lot, telling them how backbreaking it was just trying to stay ahead of the shoppers' demands for a cart. "I needed a blow dryer some evenings to melt the ice on 'em." And then he'd lead the jeers when his father Dan would try to tell them how much harder gathering shopping carts was in his day, before the invention of the shopping cart wheel.

Jeff had risen through the ranks of FCI steadily after his schooling. He was too modest to ever tell anyone or point out his progress to his father, but Dan knew through trusted people like RJ and Peter that Jeff was effective and a good fit for FCI's future. Without some of Jeff's innovations in the supply chain and various plant floors' separating and processing equipment layout, FCI wouldn't have found the kind of scalability required to maintain the customer experience shoppers had come to expect over several decades.

"Boy, it sounds like you have your hands full this week," said Inge pensively, debating whether she should drop the Jimmy bombshell, with Jeff on such a high. She knew Jeff had a heart of gold and how empathetic he was when he heard troubling news. He wouldn't sleep well if he heard her story.

"When's Jennifer going to be back, Jeff?" she said, a little too quickly.

"Oh, she's with her sisters. I told her I can handle the fort here and to use the time with her sisters and enjoy it. I think they're booked for some spa visits up there tomorrow and the day after. They'll have a great time. I know you're always busy, Inge, but you should have gone, too."

"Sounds fun. I should have," she said softly, her voice starting to break.

Jeff must have sensed that there was more to this evening call than just chit chat about his family life and broke in abruptly. "Ing, what is the matter? Oh, God—is it Dad again? Is he sick? Has it returned?"

"No, Jeff, Dad and Mom are fine. It's Jimmy. He's going down a bad path." And she recounted for her older brother the day's events. When she was done, the phone was silent and the quiet continued for an interminably long time.

"Jeff? Jeff, are you there?"

"I am here, Ing. Wow. This will be awful for Mom and Dad to find out, but we have to help him."

"What are you thinking?" she asked.

"Right now I have no idea, and I've got an eight year old looking after a baby, so I have to go. But let me think on it."

Big Trouble

Dan was halfway through his coffee the following morning when his cellphone buzzed with a text. Texting was new to him and he had only agreed to carry the phone after succumbing to unrelenting pressure from Marnie and the family. Did it make him more or less effective, he wondered? His thinking was that perhaps back in the old days the sender would have been compelled to think for himself and the extra communication would have been unnecessary.

Putting his glasses on, he scanned through what was sent. Fed up with loss of acuity with his vision, Dan had had laser eye surgery a few years back. Compared with some friends at his club, his experience had been fairly benign. In the end, he was surprised and pleased that his vision had improved so much. Now, gradually, he was noticing his near vision changing again and had gone back to keeping "readers" around.

Hmm, interesting, he thought. It was a note from Jeff. His son was generally fairly self-contained and, due to his unique set of skills, he operated on special projects within the operational side of FCI, and it was rare to get a work-related call from Jeff at a corporate level. No, Dan thought, when Jeff had a major challenge it usually went through RJ as VP of operations before, and if, it ever got to Dan. Something must be up, he decided.

He opened the text and saw that it was a simple text asking him to check his personal email account. He made a mental note to remember to do it when he got to the office. But that would have to wait, as right now, he was late for meeting with a mechanic, who was in the middle of a major overhaul on the floats and hydraulics on his plane.

The trip to the airfield was uneventful, and he listened to the morning news on the radio as he drove. The announcer came on and the lead morning story was of a planned crackdown by the mayor on some of the street activity in the city's inner core. In the interview, the mayor was quoted as saying that while there was no cause for alarm, parts of the downtown were being infiltrated by criminal elements. Only half listening, thinking it didn't really concern him, Dan considered what he knew of the mayor.

That guy is always saying the sky is falling, he thought, although he realized that he and the mayor had totally different responsibilities in life and, as the Fortune estate was just outside the city limits, he didn't have a chance to elect this mayor anyway.

He also had no business interest in the inner city, as the FCI business model had been one of following Curtis Development into new planned community developments, which had gradually ringed this city and any population center of reasonable size in that part of the country. Until urban renewal started to be looked at in the core, it was not going to be on the FCI radar at all. It was a long way away, and he figured that would be someone else's decision by then anyway.

Just then he heard the announcer refer to Remington Heights. Why does that place sound so familiar? I wonder what's going on there.

The voice on the radio continued. "In an interview after yesterday's press conference on urban issues, the mayor admitted to this reporter that he felt the police service may be losing the battle in several areas, including the recently gentrified Remington Heights neighborhood."

"We thought we had cleaned up the problems in RH. Now we find that some of this city's undesirable elements are busy reclaiming it as their own," the mayor said with grim resignation.

Remington Heights? Wasn't that Jimmy's neighborhood? Why he felt the need to be down there was beyond Dan's understanding. Dan knew his son had needed to make his own way. Dan also knew about starting out close to the bottom and figured it was a good move for his youngest.

He figured the situation would work itself out over time. The cops just needed to put their foot down and remove the bad guys, he thought to himself. Still, a sense of unease swept over Dan as he started to form a dark picture in his mind, filled with the "what ifs" of Jimmy living in that area.

Just then the phone rang, which cut off the radio. Seeing Marnie's cell number come up on the screen, he pushed the talk switch. "Hi. What are you doing?" she asked.

"Same as every day. Heading to work, but I won't get there for another hour. I'm stopping by to see how the plane's coming along," he said.

"Have you got the time to talk, Dan?" said Marnie, her expressive voice coming over the speaker phone.

"Um." He was already mentally transporting from this conversation and thinking about the plane.

"Dan!! Focus, I'm trying to talk with you."

"Yes, sorry about that. Okay, I'm listening."

"Dan, something's wrong with our family and I can't really figure it out. Between Fanny causing the crises she usually has going at work and with Al, and Inge not moving her life forward beyond being an area socialite, I am concerned. And when's the last time you heard from your sons? I never hear from Jeff, or Jimmy for that matter, and I can see what we've built in our family fraying apart. I just don't like the way things are going right now for us."

Dan listened, knowing that Marnie needed to be heard beyond anything else, and when something caused her to show this kind of concern, it was usually for a good reason.

"Well, it just so happens I heard from Jeff this morning," Dan said, trying to calm his wife a bit.

"You did? What did he want?"

"I don't know. He just said to check my email when I get in, so I assume he's immersed in something and may be overstepping his budgetary bounds with RJ. I'm sure he wants to bounce it off me in case he needs support. Some of his best innovations for us have involved some extra investment. Maybe he just wants to talk it through with me?"

A long pause enveloped the phone call and Dan felt the need to ask, "Marnie are you still there?"

She took a moment to answer and finally replied, "Still here. Dan, I still think we have a problem. I'm looking at my cell and I see I got the exact same text from Jeff. What if it's one of the kids or Jennifer? I'm feeling strange on this and I don't know why," she continued, and he knew she was settling in to a mode where a long talk was going to happen.

Dan arrived at the hanger and saw the aviation crew just getting the shop open for the day. He interrupted his wife, slightly irritated with the direction she was taking their conversation. "It's probably nothing, honey. Let me get to my office and I'll contact him and see what's going on." Seeing the mechanic advancing on his car, he quickly said goodbye and hung up.

Back in her dressing room at home, Marnie closed her eyes, somewhat hurt by her husband's curt manner. She was meeting friends that morning for a day shopping for evening gowns for an upcoming event and tried to turn her attention back to looking through what she would wear for the day's shopping trip.

She thought back to her late father and how he liked to quote life lessons to her and her sisters and she recalled the one about houses divided not standing. Did her own family understand that principal? Did they have enough affinity for each other? Had the family's success somehow turned to divide them and cause their ultimate downfall? Why did she feel this way and why was she now starting to feel herself break out into a sweat?

"There's something wrong and I have to get to the bottom of it," she said aloud as she looked around her closet.

Just then she heard a phone call coming in. It rang several times as she leaned back against the wall, trying to will the phone to cease ringing. Eventually it did stop. Ester, the Fortunes' long-time housekeeper, came into the room with the phone. "It's for you, Mrs. Fortune. It's Mrs. Martin. She's wondering if you'd like to ride with her today."

Marnie took the phone. "Hi, Mary. How nice of you to think of me. Of course we're still on for today. I can't wait. I'm really looking forward to getting together. Did I hear from Ester that you'll be driving?" And then, using a skill she had called on for years, Marnie engaged her friend in a cheerful conversation about a trip Mary had recently taken. She was careful to keep it light and not betray her previous angst and doubts.

The Boss

The FCI corporate offices were in full swing for the day and the parking lot was almost filled with employees' vehicles when Dan arrived later that morning. He had parked at his traditional spot, which was unassigned and at the far end of the lot. Old habits die hard, and Dan was never going to allow any preferred parking designations beyond those for the handicapped and business visitors to the corporate building. His rule on this was the same on all FCI properties.

He felt he learned more from that walk up to the entry doors than during other parts of his day. He noticed who was in and who wasn't, and he was able to gauge the general appearance of the place. He tried to see it through the eyes of a visitor. He'd heard somewhere that this was part of the principle of *reflection*: it's often only when you looked specifically for things such as dead foliage or cigarette butts without looking at anything else that you could spot exactly what you focused on.

In this way he was known to the grounds-keeping staff as having an uncanny eye for the details of the properties. It kept them on their toes and they tried even harder to make sure the corporate offices of FCI were in pristine shape, no matter the season. As he said when he talked to management staff, the experience people have in this building should extend to every square foot of the production facilities, warehouses and retail locations.

The quality of the customer's experience was something Dan had never taken for granted. Even through the years as the business grew much larger, he never let up on ensuring the goal remained to exceed people's expectations.

Walking in, he greeted those he knew by name and those he didn't with an upbeat "Good morning." He headed right to his office and asked his assistant Miss Tibbs to join him, as was their regular routine. They'd been together a long time and she knew her boss's habits and principal concerns innately.

She always insisted on calling Dan "Mr. Fortune." He had asked that she call him Dan back when she started 30-plus years ago, but she liked a bit of formality between them and so it was "Mr. Fortune" and "Miss Tibbs." Tibbs had never married, and back in the old days would have been referred to as a spinster, but it wasn't the old days and she was just unmarried.

They went through the daily routine of all the information that had come in overnight, such as individual store revenues and a look at the current actual cash flows for each component of the FCI empire. The stores were the most important piece to him, and he liked to look at the comparisons between location projections and the actual numbers; it read like a story to him.

A great deal of the shipped product was fresh. It required an accounting system that was more exacting, as payables and receivables were executed on demand.

He didn't waver from looking it all over and appreciated that Miss Tibbs encapsulated the information that was most important to him. After they had gone through it all, his assistant moved toward the door. She turned around and Dan sensed she had something important to ask, so he sat back from the screen in front of him.

"Mr. Fortune, I know we're really busy here right now, but could I possibly take next Friday afternoon off?" She continued, "I'd like to attend a college graduation. I'm the great aunt of twin boys, and they're both finishing school. Our family is attending the ceremony and having a celebratory dinner afterwards."

"Miss Tibbs, you know that family is everything to us here. Of course you will be there. College is a big achievement. Is that Paul and Pete who worked for us over at the Clearview store as teenagers?"

"Yes it is, sir. Thanks for remembering them. It wasn't easy for the family financially. However, the employee bursaries they accessed through FCI were a godsend, and I helped out financially as well."

"What an accomplishment!" Dan smiled. When he heard about graduations and commencements like Tibbs would be attending, he often thought about the one he didn't get a chance to attend: his own.

Then his face changed as he thought about Jimmy never pursuing any schooling beyond high school. Marnie and Dan still hoped he would try higher education, but he hadn't decided on a direction yet. School might not be an option, Jimmy had often told them.

"You really shouldn't be thinking that way for me," their youngest would tell them if they pushed it.

"Miss Tibbs, you really can't miss that. Enjoy the moment with your family. I will mark it in. I may be off that day myself as I think the overhaul on my plane is just about completed and I would like to take it up to the lake. That day would be as good as any," he told her.

Tibbs retired to her outer office and Dan was turning his attention back to work that was on his desk when his assistant called back in through the open door and said, "By the way, did Jeff get a hold of you yet? He called here this morning just as I arrived. He sounded insistent that you find some time for him today."

That reminded Dan to look at his private email and responded with a chuckle to Miss Tibbs. "That Jeff is probably on to a new idea and wants my backing before he springs it on the executive team."

He read through some internal FCI memos and then noticed the new email from Jeff.

From: JFortune@FCI.com

To: DanFortune_priv@FCI.com

Dad

Trying to get hold of you and wondered if we could get together later today and discuss something that's important to our family. It's about Jimmy and I think it has to be addressed. I'm inviting Fanny and Inge as well, as I think they should be there. I've asked Ester to try and track down Mom.

Can you do 4pm at your office? We will find some space where we can talk in private. If we do it there it's probably most convenient for Fanny as well. Let me know as soon as you can clear that time for us.

J

Dan thought back to previous conversations he'd had with Jeff about Jimmy and knew that Jeff espoused some strong views on his younger brother and had his own picture of what level Jimmy should have attained in life by this stage. Dan worried that getting everyone together to talk about whatever was going on was a bad idea.

He found these family situations very distracting. Hadn't they learned from what they'd gone through with his former son-in-law the bobsledder a few years back? How divisive that had been?

Everybody was always harping about Jimmy. Couldn't they just give him a chance to get through what he was working through and live and let live?

Even at this age, Dan still felt he'd been partially robbed of his youth by the untimely demise of Double F. He had vowed that things would be different for his children, that they could do what they wanted to. He knew that monetarily he had given about the same to the elder three at this point and it was helping them establish themselves in life.

Instead of the discussion they had planned, he felt that any new conversation should be about what he planned to do for Jimmy to get him off to a running start. He knew there would be lots of contradictory views on how Jimmy would use the financial means that Dan felt he needed to give his son. He also had a sense of foreboding that it would end up in a fight.

Besides, Dan liked the fact that his youngest was a bit of a free spirit. He reminded him of his own brother, Peter. Back when Double F had passed away, there were an awful lot of questions about Peter and his ability to find a direction and stick to it. Dan recalled that the person leading the charge of those worrying about Peter was Dan himself.

Peter had effectively found the necessary motivation a few days after their father had died and that motivation was due to imminent peril if the old Market had gone under. Yes, Dan thought, there's nothing like the threat of ruin to get people focused, and he found himself strangely regretful that FCI had become so stable over the years. He suspected it took an edge off his family. An edge that he knew they possessed but which was no longer very evident.

He sent Jeff a quick note to acknowledge receipt and to say he'd be waiting for everyone here. He then walked out into the outer offices toward the boardroom, where some of his marketing development people were going to be talking about strategic directions for FCI's organic food lines. He hoped he wasn't needed as these sessions could be dry, dull and far, far away from what he felt the food business was actually about.

Later that day he was driving back from the plant when his cell phone rang and he realized he was late for the family meeting. He knew it was Miss Tibbs and she would be mildly disapproving that he wasn't keeping to his schedule. He let it ring a little too long and then picked up. He heard Jeff's voice. "Dad? Are you coming?"

Dan felt a little impatient with the call and the question. Did people not realize that he was still leading a company with several hundred million dollars in annual revenue?

"Yes, I am, Jeff I just ran over time at the plant. I was walking around. Did you realize that the new system for offloading and individually boxing fresh produce can almost guarantee that the only two people to actually touch a piece of produce, like a tomato, are the laborer who picks it and the customer who eats it?"

Jeff gave a nervous laugh and said, "Yes, I do, Dad. Don't you recall that that was one of my designs for the equipment layout? You were at the Industrial Park plant, weren't you?"

"Yes I was, and we have really got something slick in the way that plant is set up. I'm going to get the people in PR to do something up for that trade magazine that's been looking to do a piece on us."

"That makes a lot of sense, Dad, but we really have to talk about Ji—."

"What a history in our company that Industrial Park operation has," Dan said, breaking in on his son without hearing the end of what Jeff was trying to say.

Jeff realized his father loved talking about the past. He knew he was now in for a "glory days" story on how it once was and so resigned himself to hearing his father out.

"I remember buying the land for that building before it was built. I thought I'd have a nervous breakdown and that my head was going to explode with the risks of not getting something up and running in time to service three new retail spots that were almost ready.

"Ben Curtis and his development team were ahead of schedule on the new space, and my agreement with CDC was always that, as anchor tenant, FCI had to be the first open in any new development. We both knew that food and people's stomachs were the big draw to get the public to change their consumer patterns and come to a new shopping center.

"Our capacity to supply new locations had to be guaranteed or I would incur penalties in our contract. I wouldn't have been able to handle the payments on empty retail space with no revenues for even 60 days at that point. Ben came through and hooked me up with the right people to build Industrial Park quickly. He really helped get me out of that bind."

"Pap's is a wonderful guy, isn't he?" Jeff said, sighing, acknowledging his father-in-law and then, almost embarrassed, added, "You're a great guy, too, Dad. It's just that Jennifer's father has been getting back to carrying on since Ginny passed away and he sits down on that island of his, just continuing to be who he has always been: a caring father to Jen and her brother and sisters, and a friend and substitute father figure that I can go to anytime if I need him. A talk with him is often all I need to get my mind around a challenge."

Dan listened to his son, feeling a bit smaller than he had at the start of the call. "Jeff, I'll be there in 10 minutes. Are we ready to go?"

"Yes, Dad. I see Inge in the outer office surrounded by all of the male managers, and Mom is here getting in the way of Miss Tibbs." He meant to sound like he was teasing, but the reduced sound quality from the Bluetooth gave his voice an air of apprehension.

"No sign of Fanny, though. She didn't acknowledge the email but she isn't real good at getting back to anyone unless there's an FCI press release to be quoted on."

"That's enough, Jeff," Dan snapped. His sharp reply was an uncharacteristic volley to Jeff's casual barb against his sister. "She's no less instrumental in getting things done in this company than you or anyone else here, Jeff. Is that clear? I have no time for infighting. I can already see what this afternoon is going to be like." He jabbed his finger forcefully toward the windshield as he made his point. Dan came to a stop at a traffic light, feeling an uncomfortable anxiety enveloping him.

Throughout his life, Dan had been a physical talker and when under stress, he used a lot of body language. Marnie had asked him years ago to spare her his histrionics when he was upset. She referred to it as his tendency to "be a little dramatic."

Marnie's late father had always talked to his daughters about the need to understand one's own personal style and try to adapt it if it was getting in the way of better communication in the family. "Girls, your biggest behavioral strengths become your biggest weaknesses when they're overused," Dr. Farver would admonish his daughters. "And that goes for everything, including not only our aggressiveness but when we're naturally too passive. We have to think before reacting with our first emotions, or we're not as effective."

Dan had worked hard to overcome this tendency, finding that it made great business sense to avoid wearing his emotions so openly. He'd thought of it as a kind of a mental brake that he applied on himself when necessary.

So it was unlike Dan to show any outward signs of stress, but he was starting to feel that things weren't quite right within his family. That included the bonds they had with each other.

Just then he looked to his left while still stopped to see a little girl in the car beside him staring intently at him through the closed window. Dan knew he looked foolish with his mime rant and he broke his gaze and stared forward.

"I'll be right there." After a pause, he asked, "Jeff are you still on the line?" but it was dead. Then, not knowing whether his cell had dropped the call or Jeff had hung up on him, he drove ahead once the light turned green.

He regretted their short conversation. He knew that Jeff was by nature a problem solver, whether about an engineering function or about people. His response to either was always the same: he tried to identify the facts early and then didn't let too much time pass between identifying the problem and moving toward a solution. Dan supposed his response had gotten

Jeff's back up, and he promised himself he'd be more conciliatory when they all met at the office.

The doctor who'd treated him during his brush with prostate cancer had asked him during the diagnostic stage about whether he felt unduly stressed during his day-to-day business affairs. Dan had denied feeling stress and said surely there must be many other people with a great deal more stress than him. "Doctor, I have absolutely no financial worries," he'd said, thinking back to the days when personal cash flow was a more imminent concern.

"Did I mention money, Dan?" the doctor said.

"Well, I guess you didn't, but I just assumed that was where you were going. I read somewhere that money is very high on the list of what causes people stress. Surely everyone's concerned about money?" said Dan.

"Yes, I've read something like that, too, but not feeling in control of your destiny is always number one on those lists, and that one covers people of all different means." He went on to say that people responded to stress in a variety of ways and that stress could be compared to weight gain. "Most people are comfortable in a certain weight range," he said, "and in the same way, a certain stress load." Then snapping his fingers, he added, "But all of a sudden they see themselves in a photograph or in a passing mirror and notice that they aren't as trim as they thought they should be and start to mentally compensate through dieting, exercise or—"

"—buying bigger clothes?" Dan asked.

"Yes, I suppose some of us do," the doctor said, smiling. "But Dan, stress is a little different. Often, you can't change your situation. The only thing you can change is how you choose to deal with it."

Finally caving in to the truth he'd been avoiding, Dan finished their visit saying, "That's what everybody's been saying: You'll feel better, and not to worry and that this is all fine, and it's not."

Back at his office now, Dan found a spot, still parking toward the back even though those who'd come in early and already finished for the day, like the produce buyers, had created room near the front doors.

Remembering that conversation with his physician, he thought about how, today, he must be adding to his stress load by the minute.

He sat in his car for a while, thinking of the conversation with his son, and then moved on to Ben, Jimmy and a bunch of other things. Thinking about all these concerns at once perplexed him, and he realized that—for once—he didn't have a plan.

Avoidance

Dan was deep in thought as he walked from the parking lot to the front entrance, so deep he didn't see an obvious cigarette butt just off the walkway. Dan hated himself for feeling resentful of Ben's relationship with Jeff and knew that part of his reaction on the phone was a feeling that Marnie was right and that his family was unravelling in some way. He felt a pained acknowledgment that he wasn't like his friend Ben, who always knew how to handle these types of situations. He ascribed to Ben a special personal magic that even to this day Dan had never really figured out.

Marnie had described this after Ginny's memorial; to her, Ben was what true success looked like. He had his values in complete alignment with how he approached life, including business. He was one of the people she could count on one hand whose legacy and business interests could go forward in his family. She imagined when he died, hopefully one faraway day, he would die happy with what he had created.

Dan knew the Curtises were on the 100 List as one of the country's wealthiest families. Even though Ben tried to stay under the radar, those in the business press were always interested in his views on the economy.

He was well known to them as "a good quote" and someone who got to the point when he was asked to comment. Those media members he had confidence in could count on a fiscally conservative opinion and predictions that came close to reality when they asked about cyclical business situations and where the economy was headed.

He told Dan he'd moved south to his island to get out of the limelight and the obligations of being a success. "Besides," he told Dan, "my kids have got it handled now. They don't need me looking over their shoulder. They have so many ideas of their own that me being in the room when a plan is being hatched is detrimental. If I'd been thinking, I would have grabbed that son of yours to join our business. Jeff is so solid, Dan, and a testament to both you and Marnie as parents. It's like he understands what we went through way back when we got it all started. Like he was a fly on the wall or something. I'm glad he works so well with you, though, and his heart is definitely with FCI, as it should be. You mean so much to him, Dan," Ben had said. "He has fathered some great looking grandkids and I have to say he was probably the perfect match for Jennifer. He lets her set her own direction, and she needs that to be able to utilize her smarts in her own way."

In casual conversations, Dan had learned that Jennifer was thinking ahead and, after her child raising years were behind her, she wanted to spend some of her time working with the Curtis Foundation. She thought she could contribute by helping manage the family's efforts and supporting projects to ensure they remained aligned with the thinking of the second and third generations of her family.

A long distance phone call he had with Ben after he had decided to spend most of his time on his island interrupted his thoughts again. "They tell me the development business is changing, Dan, and it's not a game for old coots like us anymore. There was a time when we knew immigration would drive people toward us and fill my developments and your grocery stores. But now we're headed into the very places that many of the people who immigrated to our country came from.

"Those people who've done well in our country are now renewing and reviving their homelands with world-class facilities from the wealth they created abroad. I think in the next 50 years the real challenge will be in correct strategic thinking and planning. Kind of reading the tea leaves on where to put resources for families like the Curtises. And the Fortunes, too," he added.

Ben continued, "So far, my time down on this island has been great for giving me the emotional distance from our company. I think I have much better vision on things than I did when I was immersed in it all the time. When the family does ask me to weigh in, I feel way more effective for them, as I can be more objective just due to the distance … I'm not wrapped up in the day to day."

Dan knew, though, that the move to the island had been for a very different reason altogether for Ben and his wife. He often told Dan that he and Marnie were welcome to come for a visit anytime they wished and they had taken him up on that offer a few times over the years when Ginny was still alive, but then things had changed. On their last visit, Ben had disclosed that he was afraid that Ginny's forgetfulness was something they couldn't contain anymore. She was having a hard time remembering who was who when the family got together, and Ben had wanted to shield her from any public embarrassment.

She was no longer the Grande Dame of the city's social set, even though Ben made some solo appearances on her behalf when he could for some of the causes his wife had faithfully supported. Toward the last few years of her life, the Fortunes and other close friends had known she was descending into the grips of Alzheimer's and had gradually drifted toward a far-off place from which no one—not even Ben could bring her back. Ginny Fortune had died in the way she had lived, surrounded by those she loved, about 15 months before.

Marnie had asked a few times toward the end if Dan thought it was a good idea to go down and see the Curtises, even though Ginny wouldn't know them, but Dan hadn't wanted to go. He rationalized with Marnie that they would be in the way. He realized, though, that deep inside he hadn't yet come to grips with his own mortality and the eventuality of something similar happening to either him or Marnie. Having a tough situation right in his face was something he thought he wouldn't be able to bear to see. He still held out a prideful hope that the question for him would be "if he died" and not "when he died."

Prior to her mother's death, Jennifer and Jeff had got down when they could to see Ginny and came back with troubling reports about her ever-accelerating decline. Marnie and their daughter-in-law had several long talks that had helped Jennifer reconcile her emotions with what was happening. It was a struggle for Jennifer to watch this happen to her beloved mother, someone to whom she knew she owed everything she had become in life. How could she pay back that kind of love? This question and others swirled in her head when she would have to come back home and be a mother to her own small children.

As the Curtis family gathered to say goodbye, Jeff had thought of the answer she sought, as they shared tea just outside the room where Ginny would die later that morning.

"Mom would be very happy with what you're doing already. You're the one of all of us who's least touched by station. She's taking her body with her to the last, but her better self, her love for everyone, she can't take with her. She has left it for you to carry on as her legacy."

Her father Ben had established a full-time care facility for his wife on a property that was right in their compound, and his plan was to turn it over to the island government after she passed away, as an urgent care facility. Once it had been readied and even when Ginny was still alive, he'd made an arrangement with all the villages along the coast to have inoculation days for those who wanted and needed them. Ben watched his wife a lot through the day. He wondered what she must think on days when she saw a line-up of local people outside her window waiting patiently to see the medical staff.

He knew she would have loved to know that they could provide something of value to the local people. It comforted him a lot, though, to think that on those line-up days she had a trace of a smile and a little life in her eyes. The doctor told him this was just a muscular reaction to the disease. But Ben preferred to believe it was something else—trying to break out of the shackles of what was slowly killing her and acknowledging and empathizing with others who ailed.

In the end, after a talk with his family, Ben disclosed his plan to fund a substantial endowment in perpetuity through the Curtis Foundation.

Their shared vision was that the clinic could be permanently staffed by at least one doctor and other medical staff, to provide the local people with a medical center to call their own.

Dan reflected on all of this and wondered if he had it in him to create a legacy that made sense for the next generations of the Fortune family. One step at a time, Fortune, he told himself. You have to get through this meeting first and then maybe there will be a way forward.

Putting all this out of his mind, he strode up the staircase toward the FCI executive suites with the sense that the Fortunes were all in for a tough conversation this evening.

Miss Tibbs had booked the boardroom and directed Inge, Jeff and Marnie to a seat, saving the one at the head of the table for Dan. He took note that Fanny hadn't made it and wondered why.

Taking his spot, he looked around the room and guessed that whatever was wrong, the other three had already started without him, as he saw the unmistakable look of anguish in his wife's eyes. Her eyes were a bit red and it appeared that she was close to tears.

They got started on a discussion that he would remember for the rest of his life.

The Fortune Huddle

Miss Tibbs closed the doors on the boardroom so that the Fortunes could have some privacy for what she surmised was a serious discussion. She couldn't recall them ever having met as a family at FCI.

Jeff got things started. "Jimmy's in trouble. Very serious trouble."

Dan tried to keep an even tone. "And why isn't Jimmy here to tell us himself about the trouble he's supposedly in?"

The others shifted uncomfortably in their chairs as Dan spoke, his voice revealing the stress he was feeling and hardly sounding like himself. "Have I not said to all of you over the years that back-hall chatter isn't fair? I went through years of this kind of crap as a kid, with Double F blowing up and my mother trying to placate him. It was nonsense." His voice rose. "He would come home from the Market and have all kinds of arguments going on in his mind with the townspeople or some of the staff, and I always guessed that most were unfounded.

"The other people probably didn't even know there was a problem and he would gradually shut them all out and not even bother to speak to them. He made so many enemies in that town from just not knowing how to confront problems that he died without a close friend and without even his own family—his brothers and a sister, my two uncles and my aunt—bothering to show up for his funeral. If he'd just taken the time to learn how to address things properly, most matters would have been resolved. My mother just made excuse after excuse."

The room had gone very quiet during his outburst and everyone looked down or away from Dan. Their body language showed there was trouble. Marnie, who was tearing up, broke into the conversation quietly and said, "Dan I think you should listen to Jeff."

Jeff turned to his father and started to speak. "Dad, Inge called me about some trouble she had with Jimmy at the art gallery and the ceremony for the hall space that we—you and Mom—donated to. I was going to try and get us all together anyway, as the scene Jimmy caused there was troubling to her and to me when I heard it. Then this morning I received a really difficult and troubling call from a Detective Jacobs."

Uneasily, Jeff continued. "From what I understand, he's with the plainclothes drug squad downtown and is a colleague of Mike Simons. Mike knows me well and has played on my rec league team for a few years. Mike told Jacobs to reach out to our family through me."

Dan slumped back in his chair and caught his wife's eyes briefly before moving back to his son, wondering where Jeff was going on this.

"I was going to try and handle this myself, or with Inge as she was the one who filled me in first that we might have a problem. I thought I'd try, but the call was a serious heads up from Detective Jacobs about Jimmy, and it involves illegal drugs."

"Well, out with it. What the hell is going on here?" Dan said, his voice betraying his fear.

"What I was told is that the undercover unit had been watching a group that's been operating in the downtown core and they'd gone to Jimmy's condo and been inside," Jeff replied. "There was a sweep last night, and Jimmy was taken into custody with the rest. He's in a holding cell at city right now."

"He's dealing dope? I don't believe you. These clowns wouldn't know a drug dealer if one showed up at their station with a pant load of the stuff and a hole in his pocket. Who else knows about this?"

"So far I don't think it's public knowledge, but if the press hears about it we're going to see our name splashed in the headlines. You know the mayor wouldn't mind showing the public he's dealing with the problems in the city core, and the press would like it if they had a familiar name in the mix," Jeff continued.

"Well, that's just great!"

Marnie jumped to the door to make sure it was fully closed.

"I spend my whole life building up a good name, and a little mistake—an unproven allegation—can harm our reputation? I'll sue any paper who prints this crap," he said.

The four of them went back and forth for another twenty minutes, arguing about what should be done. Dan felt a wave of despair washing over all of them and felt he had to make a point—any point—to get them engaged in thinking of a way to resolve this, but couldn't get his mind or his voice going.

The room went silent, all of them alone in their thoughts. The silence continued for what seemed too long. Dan glanced at the downcast faces of his family and was about to speak when, after a quick tap on the door, in walked Fanny with her ear pressed to her cellphone and obviously in harsh discussion with someone.

"Julie, you are not to go home tonight before I have that report. I need it for my meeting in the morning. What? ... I can't help you with that, Julie. You've known that I needed it since after lunch. Get it done." She clicked the phone off, leaving her assistant in midsentence.

Shaking her head at the nonsense she had to work through at FCI, she scanned the boardroom for a chair. In that brief moment, she quickly registered that something was going down. The room had gone silent. Above all, Fanny hated life's extended pauses.

"Well, why are we here? Jeff, you called this meeting. I still have a bunch of things to get done around here today and the community foundation fundraiser is tonight and I told Al to be over here to get me at 6:30 sharp. What's so damn important that we had to meet without notice?"

Jeff started to shift forward in his chair to do battle with his older sibling. "Fanny, I really hate to get in the way of your daily power trip, but the rest of us are trying to stop a shit-storm that will be extremely bad news for FCI and our family. Damaging for all the Fortune families: yours, mine, this one, Uncle Peter's and our cousins'. I might add that we were all here on time to see if we can fix this and we don't—"

"Oh, come on, Jeff. Don't give me your wimpy Mr. Fix-it act in this room. You haven't got all your adoring line workers watching."

Inge tried to break in. "Fan, stop. This isn't helpful. Jimmy's in trouble. He's in jail."

Fanny, her jaw dropped open, eyebrows raised, immediately saw aspirations of a political career go up in a faint flicker of smoke that she knew would soon be a forest fire. Angered, she responded the only way she knew how, and lashed out. Strangely, Fanny found that conflict had a calming effect on her, and the resultant adrenaline rush was a fuel that somehow made her feel good. Unfortunately, most other people found themselves repelled at her style, which was the main reason she couldn't get a lot done through other people.

Fanny fought for air as she swivelled her chair around to the end of the table where Dan and Marnie sat looking completely spent. "Jail? Well maybe he just didn't get enough dirtbikes as a boy, Dad."

Marnie, seeing the situation careening out of control, spoke softly and slowly. "Fanny, don't speak to your father in that tone. He doesn't deserve that."

Meeting her mother's direct gaze, she fixed her eyes. "Mom, you are as much to blame as anyone here, always helping him not face up to the results of his actions. Dad was a CEO, not a father. He was never there and when he was, he pandered to Jimmy with gifts and toys. You were both always there for Jimmy like a security blanket."

Fanny continued. "How many times did you get involved in his education to move him around to other schools because you thought he was getting poor results because of the teachers or because the kids he was trying to hang with weren't up to your standards? As far as I can see, this is much more your mess than it is anyone else's." As Fanny finished, she felt that familiar exhilaration coming over her in waves, with the conflict now in full flame.

Fights and arguments have a way of turning even the most timid of bystanders into active agitators, and a crowd mentality was seeping into this situation. Emboldened to speak out by her much more aggressive sister's rant, Inge recounted what had happened at the opening of the art gallery. She didn't spare any of the details of Jimmy's actions and stopped when she noticed her parents looking at one another in shocked bewilderment.

Jeff sat with his head in his hands as he thought about what this conversation meant for them all. There was now a crack in their family and he wondered if opening it in this dramatic fashion was anything but a terrible mistake on his part.

Fanny now couldn't help herself. "If that little prick thinks he's ever welcome around his niece and nephew again he has another thing coming. I can't be bothered with him. He'll probably be trying to turn them on to drugs, if he gets a chance."

Marnie was now openly sobbing, her tears running down. "Oh, God, no. Stop it all of you!"

Suddenly Dan, in a fit of pique, slammed both his fists on the table, his face red with rage, and said, "That's all, goddammit. That's all I want to hear out of any of you. We've tried and given all we could. Building this place was hard. What we've done we did for all of you. Maybe I was gone a lot but I always came back, didn't I?

"Every time I left, it was for the betterment of everyone in this family, and every time I came back it was for this family. We're in a crisis here and

I don't know what the hell to do but I will not have you speaking to either of us in this way. We are not bad people."

With that, Dan Fortune walked to the door and, just before opening it, said, "Now get yourselves together. There's an office full of people outside this boardroom that count on this family for their living, and we don't need anyone thinking we are a bunch of screw-ups. It'll be bad for business.

"Jeff, go get your coat. We're going to get Jimmy out of there tonight. The rest of you wait by your phones—we might need to do some damage control."

Dan strode out, his face hardened against the stares he received from those wondering just what had happened to cause the loud voices coming from the boardroom.

Dan closed the door to his own inner office after shooing away Tibbs. He collapsed in one of the leather wingbacks at his small meeting table and started to weep, thinking of what this meant to all of them. He never thought the children would turn on him like that. They didn't know what bad parenting looked like. They'd never known Double F.

He wondered if something he'd once heard was now coming true, that eventually we all become our parents. He thought back to what had just happened in the boardroom. Were his actions not something his father would have done? He closed his eyes and muttered, "Christ, Jimmy, what have you done?"

Jeff cracked the door ajar just enough to be heard and said softly, "Dad, are you ready to go or do you need a few minutes?"

"No, now, Jeff. We do this now."

Regaining his composure, Dan grabbed his coat and descended the stairs out to the main doors and pushed through the darkness a few steps behind his son.

Neither said a word. Each lost in his own thoughts, they continued on the unfamiliar journey to the lockup where Jimmy was being held.

Part III

Ben's Island

Ben Curtis ambled down to the sea from his hilltop house. The cove was calm on the leeward side of the island, where float planes landed, away from the heavier swells of the Caribbean. Ben always felt a bit uncomfortable when the airplane had to land in anything more than a ripple. He'd received a call a few minutes earlier that a seaplane was approaching from the north. Right on time, he thought with a quick glance down at his watch. The incoming plane was a regular run that brought supplies and occasional visitors in from the mainland.

As he descended the moderately steep, rock strewn path, he was careful to avoid any areas that his balance and a new artificial hip might give him trouble with. Ben knew his doctor wouldn't have liked him putting a strain on his latest surgical repair, but he told himself he should get down to meet the visitors; these particular visitors were dear old friends.

Dan had called him nine or 10 days before and asked if he and Marnie could come down for a visit. "We'd like to come and see you, Ben. I'm not sure how long we can stay, but if you could put us up for a couple days it would be appreciated. Just some time away would be a godsend at this point."

"Put you up? You're not going to tell me you're broke, are you Dan?" Ben said laughing. "Wait—if you're broke, I might be, too." He roared down the phone line at his own humour.

Dan on the other end of the line could visualize the fun that Ben was having with the premise, but didn't feel the mirth quite as much as his old friend did. His eyes were fixed on the wall map in front of him in his office. While Ben's spot was actually much too small to be recognized officially on the map, someone had drawn a cartoon of it onto the map in a vacant blue patch of water. A little mound rising out of the blue with a solitary palm tree and what looked like a balding castaway with a shaggy beard reading a book. Underneath, carefully lettered, was BEN'S ISLAND. Marnie had covertly drawn it on the map a few years ago, after a visit. Every time Dan looked at that map and saw Marnie's graffiti, he wondered if she was trying to send him a message

"I think we have enough points to get us both down there for nothing," he countered, knowing that Ben loved to poke fun about how he now lived in paradise and Dan still hadn't given up control of FCI. As he waited for the assurance that Ben was OK with a visit, he daydreamed about somehow snapping his fingers and finding himself standing on the deck of Ben's beautiful getaway. To Dan, the view of that lookout, so high over the lush tropical flora growing on every square inch of the island rivaled anything he'd ever seen.

Ben had reminded his old friend that the Fortunes had a standing invitation since he'd first developed the island, and it would be his pleasure. He'd figured that something was weighing heavily on them both, but didn't give away that he'd been expecting the Fortunes to call about visiting.

Of course, he'd been talking to his daughter Jennifer and did have an inkling of what might be on his friends' minds. She'd told him Jeff's whole family was in chaos over the thing with Jimmy, and that the mudslinging back and forth was getting terrible.

Ben absorbed his daughter's upset right down the phone line. "I've never seen Jeff so miserable. It's like witnessing a building on fire and its owners are standing on the sidewalk watching and not moving to call the fire department."

He listened thoughtfully and without interruption. At the end of the call, he just said, "Jen, these things get worked out. As we both know, the Fortunes are a wonderful family. They'll get through this and all you can do is be part of the solution and not add to the problem. Be there for Jeff, but also for young Jimmy. He's going to need to know he matters."

His aging eyes were now transfixed on the tip of the island that jutted out to the sea. There was a glint of sunlight. From the tail, perhaps, he thought. Then he could see the seaplane coming around on its approach to the cove. He took a breath, holding it as he always did as it skipped once, twice and then three times before breaking the flat tension of the water for good; the pontoons pulled into the surface to start slowing down the aircraft for a safe landing.

Ben thought back to the time he first met Dan at the store. It seemed so long ago and he remembered how rigid Dan had been; he'd focused on what he considered his principal mission and burden: taking on the original Fortune Family Market, paying down the debt he'd inherited from his father and then settling into town life as a simple grocer.

Ben wondered if Dan had lost sight of the fact that changing that initial vision was what had allowed him to have the victories he experienced in his life with FCI, how getting out of his own way had allowed Dan to achieve what was well within his capability.

Did the Fortunes understand that victories came not only in business? That personal victories in home and family life were the ultimate reason why success could feel as good as it felt?

As he watched, the plane taxied up to the dock. In the rear window, hands waved. Right then, he made up his mind that if they wanted to tell him about their situation, they could. If not, he'd try to ensure that they had some respite from their day to day and had a good time, leaving relaxed.

Some of the staff from the house had arrived earlier in the estate's vehicles. Now, as the pilot taxied the plane toward the berth at the shoreline, they signaled him to cut the engine and allow the plane to ease over so it could be lashed down to the side of the dock to allow the guests to disembark.

The Fortunes stepped down and looked around, orienting themselves to their new surroundings. Ben was already over to the plane and attempting to get his head inside to inspect the supplies that had been flown in.

He told the compound staff to make sure the medical supplies and cases of infant formula weren't buried in the material as it was unloaded. These, he reminded them, were needed right away at the infirmary. This building had been retrofitted more completely after his wife passed away. It was now finally set up as Ginny had wanted—a full-time medical facility for the surrounding townspeople—and it was always kept busy with their needs.

Ben noticed that his guests were somewhat ill at ease with all the hoopla and, seeing their exhaustion, decided to move the group to the main house on up the hill as quickly as he could.

He then turned with a smile and exclaimed that he was delighted to reintroduce the Fortunes to all assembled, some of his dearest old friends. He quickly added they were actually in-laws and Jeff's parents. Dan gathered that most knew Jeff well due to his occasional visits with Jennifer and the grandchildren, as a wave of smiles swept through the group.

Marnie also noticed the murmurs and nods of assent when her son was mentioned and, in all the heartache she'd experienced in the previous few months, it was heartening to feel that Jeff had made an impact on people here on Ben's island.

A Range Rover quickly pulled up onto the dock, and all the luggage was loaded, with Dan and Marnie sliding into the back seat for the journey up the winding road to the estate. At the same time, an ancient flatbed truck was backed in close to the seaplane's cargo hatch so they could unload the cargo.

Ben took a last look at what supplies had arrived and then, with his cane, levered himself onto the SUV's running board. With a final push from the driver, he found his way through the front passenger door and onto the seat.

He turned to the Fortunes and reassured them with a smile and a wink, saying, "Isn't it hell getting old?"

At that statement of truth, the vehicle lurched forward up the road and everyone let out a laugh. The Fortunes especially appreciated the levity, and they started to decompress from the day of travel. They briefly left behind the feeling of despair they'd brought along as a companion.

Fore!

Dan and Marnie said nothing to Ben over the first two days on the island about the reasons they'd had to escape from the home front for a bit. There hadn't really been any time for a conversation like that, as Ben and his people squired the couple around the island to look at the various improvements they'd made to the development since they last visited.

The Fortunes were astounded to see the level of innovation Ben and his small crew had used to ensure that the compound offered most of the creature comforts good living demanded. As Marnie swam in the solar-heated pool just off the guest quarters late one evening, she decided that these amenities were that much more valued in such a remote setting. The infinity pool seemed to be invisibly elevated out over the valley floor if viewed from any vantage point from the main house. With a waterfall splashing down into the far end, it seemed as though it was just part of a pristine tropical grotto and a waterway to a far-off Shangri-La.

The next morning, in the quiet serenity of the first tee at GinBen Links, there was a distinct PING as Ben's tee shot came off his club and sailed up the fairway. Not that far, but straight. Ben had been an avid golfer for most of his life. When he'd envisioned the island's development and his estate, he'd made sure to put in a nine-hole layout. "Not bad for an old guy," he muttered aloud to an otherwise preoccupied Dan.

Ben and Ginny had always loved to remind family and friends that they were the only two permanent members at GinBen. They made sure when visitors came down to give them honorary memberships, complete with a few gag gifts like golf shirts with mock official looking crests.

Marnie had taken a pass on the round that morning. She'd struck up conversations with the clinic's medical staff and learned that it was the day when the doctor from a nearby island came for a biweekly visit. Marnie wanted to volunteer with the doctor as she checked up on the progress of a few of the local women who'd be giving birth in the following months. She'd told the two men at breakfast and then took the short walk over to the medical facility to wait for Dr. Sheba, as the medical staff called her.

Dr. Sheba Ramparsad was originally from Trinidad and had received her medical education from the University of the West Indies. UWI had accepted her application under one of the original Curtis Foundation Scholarships. She'd been Ben's first attempt at supporting UWI's medical program after he'd become personally interested in taking the clinic from a care center for his wife to what both he and Ginny wanted it to become.

Sheba knew she wouldn't have been able to get her degree without Ben's support and felt that the trip to the island once a week was the least she could do for all he and Ginny had done for her. Besides, she reminded herself, that island was a microcosm of social and physical well-being. She could watch her efforts as the years passed, seeing the local people respond to a regimen of preventative medicine that many places in the world took for granted.

More recently, Ben had tasked Sheba to look out for other UWI medical students that might want to come to the island for short internships, where they could see a facility like his in action. His vision was to give other people who were looking to fund worthy causes a model of possibility. Locally trained physicians might like to consider a career that allowed them to stay in the area after graduation. As development occurred in the Caribbean, taking care of those people and their families who had careers within smaller places like his would be important.

He had told Sheba that while the geography in this part of the world was beautiful, its true resource was its people and he wanted to help as much as possible in his remaining years.

Seeing it was his turn, Dan dropped his phone with a frown and dug out a sleeve of balls from his bag. He was selecting one as Ben came back toward the rear of the tee deck and said, "They don't go that far anymore but golf is certainly a game I can enjoy, even at my age. I just have to fix that hip turn and I'll have another 20 yards in my tee shots."

Dan approached the tee blocks and placed a tee in the ground silently, marvelling at how his friend could even be thinking about extra yardage after his recent hip replacement. He didn't immediately respond to Ben's comments. His mind was on a message Fanny had left in the morning about an issue at one of the processing plants and the potential of an E. coli bacterial shutdown by health regulators if things weren't fixed.

The food industry as a whole had been beset with such outbreaks over the previous few years. It was a serious situation, but the industry overall had many safeguards in place. He started to reply to the email but after a second read-through noticed that the word was *potential* and not *probable*.

His first thought had been to suggest she talk to her brother Jeff, as he was in charge of FCI's production processes and probably had some input on the reliability of the report. However, he decided against that, knowing that the two had little time for each other right now. Their clashing on something this important might evolve into a bigger conflict that might start to involve other employees, who would take sides and detract from FCI performance in general.

Instead, he forwarded the message to RJ and asked her to look into the situation in detail and send him her thoughts before the day was done.

His ball now on the tee, but not as clear of mind as his golf game demanded, Dan turned on his first shot hard. He swung through with all his frustration, to see the ball leave the tee deck and head left into the lush undergrowth that ran along that side of the fairway.

"I hope you remember our rules here at GinBen. We always take a breakfast ball off the first tee and hit until we're happy. You're pretty deep in there and—trust me—the chances of locating that ball are slim to none. Have another go. We both know they make new balls every day. Let's just have fun," Ben said kindly, sensing his friend needed to settle in.

With a harrumph, Dan hustled back to the cart to grab another ball, unhappy with himself that he was letting his headspace get in the way of his game. He set up again and put the ball into play. Not with a whole lot of distance, but OK, he thought, until he could get himself sorted and regain his focus.

He hopped into the cart beside his host and off they went to their tee shot location.

Dan found the first few holes frustrating, as he was being inundated with messages from Fanny, Jeff and now RJ, detailing what was happening in the processing plant. He was struck with how strange it was that three people looking at the same thing could somehow come up with a totally different picture when they explained it to an outside party.

Fanny's saw it as a problem with some of the older line supervisors and thought it was time for new blood in the ranks. Jeff, ever the perfectionist, pointed out the need for renewal on some of the feeder lines. RJ was more circumspect and eased Dan's mind with a more measured approach to the whole situation. Yes, she wrote, there was the possibility of trouble. A regional health inspector had dropped in unannounced on the packaged meats plant and pointed out some areas that were unlikely to pass when new guidelines were announced in the months ahead.

Dan clicked forward and read RJ's message. She wrote that Fanny and Al had been out for a business dinner the evening prior with several political figures. They'd mentioned to her that some of the food industry regulations would be changing and red flags had gone off for her.

By the next day, Fanny had looked into the matter and found out about the inspector's visit and she went nuclear. She took it upon herself to turn the processing plant upside down with various threats of what might happen if FCI ever did break regulations. The employees at most of the processing facilities were much more used to interacting with the Fortune family through Jeff and perhaps Dan, from time to time.

Once she had everyone scurrying for cover, she announced to the plant manager that he'd made her late. "From now on, keep me better informed," she said, and stormed off to her hair appointment.

RJ concluded the email by asking if it wasn't Jeff's area and not Triple F's to deal with things like this. RJ's use of Fanny's nickname was a little dig at Dan, as it was a name only she and Peter had ever used. On this day, the humour behind the remark was totally lost on the CEO.

Ben had been watching his friend sit in the golf cart while he took his own shot and then pointing back at Dan's ball, asked, "You are going to hit that thing, aren't you?"

Dan made a self-conscious grimace and motioned as if to throw his smartphone as far into the foliage as it would go. His next shot had a reasonable result and ended up on the green, with Ben clapping resolutely.

"Dan, am I out here by myself today?" Ben asked. "Playing solo is fine to a point but I was hoping we were both going to enjoy this round."

Dan made an apologetic face as he lined up his putt, still preoccupied with his thoughts but now more aware that he was not fulfilling his role as a good guest. "I'm sorry, Ben. There are some things going on in my life right now that are bothering me."

"Well, get your nose out of that phone and let's have a game," Ben said, grinning. "With the auto press on the opening holes, you're already down $14. The rout is on here unless you get with it."

The pair continued on into the tropical golf course, both enjoying the rest of the morning.

A New Arrival

That evening at dinner, the conversation drifted back to the days when the Fortunes and Curtises had first met, and then onto how the friendship and business relationship had been forged. Names came up like Doug Davis, Pudge Cameron, Beth and Bob Allan and others who had been a part of the expansion years.

They also talked about the importance timing had played in their business success. "Boy, was I in the right place at the right time," Dan said, stating the obvious. The talk was light and friendly. Ben also talked about the feeling of trust they'd felt in each other for the initial projects; he raised his glass and proposed a toast to the Fortunes.

"To our families. It is my hope that you both agree that it has been enriching to all of us, far beyond the financial benefits, to have come together over the years. Ginny and I always counted as one of our great achievements that our families were joined by Jeff and Jennifer's marriage and that we share grandkids. I know both of you agree." They all clinked glasses in acknowledgement. The Fortunes were delighted to be spending time with their old friend and to have the respite from the troubles they faced within their own clan.

Marnie raised her glass once more. "I have two things I would like to toast as well. I just miss my friend Ginny so much, as I know you do, Ben. So, to Ginny. We all know you were originally heaven sent and then taken back there much too soon."

"To Virginia Curtis, then," and as they held up their glasses, Marnie noted the small tears that formed in Ben's eyes, though he kept on smiling throughout the tribute to his late wife.

Marnie told Ben it was such a pleasure to come down and see him, see what he had created and experience the clinic. "We had a very full day and one of the ladies I was worried about looked like she was going into labor as I came up for the night. Dr. Sheba, the staff and her husband are with her, but I want to go down and check on her soon.

"This final toast, though, is to Danni, our mutual granddaughter. She's nine today, and we all know what a bright, beautiful girl she is. I called her just before dinner to wish her well and, by the way, Grandpa Ben, she said she liked the painting you did for her of the island. It came in the mail today. She tells me it's a masterpiece and that she can't wait to come down next spring. Now, Ben, in all this, when did you have time to take up painting? Do you ever stop?"

"I've done a few landscapes. It's just a way to try something different, really," he told them, a little embarrassed to have that side of him revealed. "The beauty of this place compels me to try and capture it. The art is inside me and now I just have to let it out once in a while.

"I wanted to make sure I created something from me to give to Danni, something she could hold onto as a keepsake. Something I did solely for her to remember me by before it's too late and I can't do anything for her except buy something. She's a remarkable girl and is a big help to her parents with the younger children," Ben added.

Flinching at Ben's comments about buying things and, with Jimmy's problems now back in her thoughts, Marnie asked the two men to excuse her, saying she'd be back up after she checked on the expectant mother. When she left, Ben asked Dan if they should pour an after-dinner drink and retreat to the deck to enjoy the night air. Dan, perusing the last emails of the day on his phone, nodded, not quite tuned into what Ben had said, but rising to his feet, still peering at the small screen.

"Sure, let's do it," Dan replied, eyes lowered to an email.

"Let's do what, Dan? Go swimming? Jump off the deck? Catch an alligator? What are we doing here?" Ben asked.

Caught a little off guard by Ben's abrupt demeanor, Dan quickly apologized. "Sorry, Ben, I have so much on my mind with work and all, I haven't been myself. I do apologize." He shut the phone off.

Ben directed him to a deck chaise. Turning back as he made his way inside to make the drinks, Ben said, "I'm sensing you have more going on than just work issues, Dan. I'll bet you have a hundred times the work 'issues' that you had back when we first met and that most of those problems can be handled by others now if you let them. No, I think there's something else, and we are going to talk about it when I get back."

Left alone with his thoughts, Dan could hear his friend occupied with what sounded like a drink shaker. No, the emails hadn't been all about work. Most were from Jeff and Fanny cc'ing him on their ongoing dispute about the production facilities. He saw a couple from RJ in there too, as she had now found herself in the middle of the increasingly chaotic feud. Left alone, she was trying to cool things down as best she could.

There was another from Inge reporting that she'd gone to see Jimmy and that he still didn't seem quite back to normal yet. She wrote that she thought it would be good to freeze Jimmy's trust, and asked if Dan had done that. She also sent an email testing him on whether he would support a new abstract art exhibit where the artists had done paintings with various body parts. Dan shook his head with a shudder at the thought of that.

Not a single email from Jimmy, though, which Dan realized wasn't all that rare. No, he reflected, he hadn't really received a "Hey, Dad, what's up?" email from his youngest in a quite a long time.

There was the final email from the birthday girl, his granddaughter Danni, to Marnie and him, that commented on how lucky they were to be down

Fortune's Impasse

with Grandpa Ben. Dan smiled as he read the short note, and then was stopped cold by a question. "I really love my Dad, Granddad, but when are you going to let him take over from you at work? I know he would really like to." She'd added a smiley face to the end of the sentence. Ben was back on the deck. He opened their conversation by asking, "So what's your succession plan, Dan? I haven't bothered to look at our numbers on FCI's same-store sales volume in a few years, but when I last looked, your little grocery market was doing pretty well. I'm assuming you could easily do a lot less work and a lot more living if you stepped away from FCI."

Dan took a deep breath and knew that he shouldn't be upset with his older friend for the comment, but a hint of indignation was rising in him anyway.

Ben continued. "Dan, I know you've been a great operator for many years and our most successful developments were enhanced by having you and your stores involved. I've always thought of FCI as this great big inverted pyramid. You hold it all up from the bottom and then each tier of your operation supports the next level, which ends up for your customers as a superb relationship through frontline employees.

"You must consider, though, as I once had to, that you're coming to the day when you can't hold it up all by yourself any longer. And then what? Dan, I think you have all three components of a superior business valuation: your loyal customer base, your FCI product and branding, and finally your people. What you've created has tremendous value. At one time I thought you were doing it all to eventually sell out to one of the majors, but before we all knew it FCI was a major in its own right."

Dan closed his eyes and spoke slowly. "That's all great, Ben, but you just don't understand. We've done some good things in those three areas. Do I have the bench strength in FCI that it requires for me to be able to step away? Could the teams be better? I'd be crazy if I thought the status quo was going to be all I need to do. Of course, I'm happy enough with most of it. But not totally happy," he added.

"The problem here is I don't know how to properly integrate my family into my succession because I don't know where to begin. I have one child who is at this minute probably knee deep in alienating my workforce and her siblings trying to run things. She's stymied by the thought that it can be done without raising her voice. I just see all the bad and good in my father in her. And I'm scared to death of what she would do unfettered by my presence."

Ben sat back in his lounge chair and took in what he was hearing without comment. "I have one son, your son-in-law, who's a wonderful person and manager, but I don't know that I feel comfortable elevating him into my spot over his older sister. Jeff is green on too many things on the customer side. He's an engineer, for God's sake. I just can't. He needs some more rounding."

"Our beautiful Inge has too many expensive tastes for any man other than her father to be able to afford. She's either committing my money to philanthropic causes that I don't know if we should be aligned with or getting herself involved with men that I worry will eventually come to me looking for an exit payout. That Alfie cost me a lot of money. What a prince he was. The rest of the family think it cost me just a seven-figure amount to show him the door, but that didn't include the ski lodge in the Dolomites he refused to give back when it was all done. Inge is as pure as snow but she would have no problem overextending herself financially on what she's interested in if I didn't watch her like a hawk."

Ben jumped in at this point. "Dan, I wish Marnie was here to listen to this. What does she think?"

Dan confessed, "Ben I don't know that she's even paying much attention to Fanny, Jeff and Inge right now. Jimmy has gotten himself into some legal and moral troubles. We are concerned that he may also be abusing drugs. She's beside herself thinking it's because of the way we raised Jimmy, which, granted, was different from the other three."

"Who's telling you that?" Ben asked gently, seeing that Dan was unraveling before him as he disclosed the family conflict.

Fortune's Impasse

After a pause, Dan replied "Ugh ... my other three children, for starters. Let's face it, Ben. Jimmy came along when we were well into our salad days. Money was not an issue and with the travel I had in building out FCI, we dropped the ball more than once on Jimmy's upbringing. If we didn't have the time to solve what we thought was a problem, we certainly didn't think twice about throwing money at it. Marnie feels that Jimmy's current circumstances are our fault. Frankly, I feel a lot of guilt as well. We both feel we've failed him, and our other kids are piling it on."

Dan came to an abrupt stop at that point and stared off away from Ben into the impossibly starry sky. "We're in a mess, Ben, and I sure don't know how to handle this. I think we need some help. What do we do? You've been through a lot."

Ben almost surrendered to the impulse to tell Dan that he'd been aware of what was happening, but stopped himself, realizing that an opinion from him might actually hinder the Fortune family's resolution of the dilemma. Besides, he knew that if he were in Dan and Marnie's shoes, he would appreciate discretion on the matter.

When one is part of or too close to a problem, he thought, gaining clarity on what's real and what might not be fact can be an impossible task. Ben knew it was easy to box with shadows alone for a long time and that the cost, especially for a company the size of FCI, could be horrendous if issues were not addressed quickly. In circumstances like this, the most practical solution might be to call in an external resource to properly assess the situation.

Ben made a mental note to find the business contact information for a few people he could recommend. He was sure making referrals would be time well spent for Dan and Marnie to get their minds around a go-forward plan.

Ben knew that while he didn't have all the answers, many of the answers were out there, some of which the Fortunes already had within them, but didn't see yet. The issue of FCI and the need for Dan's disengagement from the day to day was the big task at hand. The infighting and

Jimmy's problems **were more symptomatic of what the first generation still needed to think through.** The central question, What is the money for? had to be addressed, and then all of the other pieces could be tackled.

The two men sat in silence for a long time. Dan, lost in his own thoughts, just stared out into the night. After clearing the table, Ben brought the glasses inside and then came out onto the deck to stand at the railing. Marveling at the absolute calm of the evening, he wondered if there was a word in any language for this exact quiet.

Just then, a blood curdling shriek emanated from down below on the grounds of the estate. The scream bellowed out with a pitch and velocity that startled Dan, and he jumped to his feet, worried for Marnie. Ben smiled resolutely and turned back, pressing his hand into his friend's chest to reassure him and holding his finger to his lips for silence.

They listened closely, and a few seconds later, they were rewarded. The scream was followed by the unmistakable mewling noise of a newborn human baby taking its first breath of this world, followed closely by a plaintive cry that pierced the stillness of the tropical night—a cry that, since time began, signified a life being started with all the promise and challenge that ultimately affects us all.

Shortly afterwards, both could hear the sheer elation in the voices of Marnie and the new father, and her delight at being part of something so uplifting.

Later that night, once the baby and mother were settled with the midwife in the clinic's makeshift nursery, an elated Marnie drifted back up the hill to the estate house. She woke Dan up to tell him about seeing the birth. She talked about her reconnection to the truth that everyone comes into the world with a blank slate and how it is what gets etched on that slate through life that's really important. He listened to her, happy that she'd been able to be so grounded by her experience, and pulled a blanket over her as she drifted off to a more comfortable sleep than she'd enjoyed in quite a while.

The next morning, before they joined Ben for breakfast, Dan told Marnie what he'd told Ben. "What did he say? Can he help us, Dan?" said Marnie.

"He has an opinion, but he believes we're better served as a family by talking with some individuals who can give us a more objective viewpoint. I go to him for many things when I'm in a bind, but he'll say he's too close. He said there are people who handle these kinds of issues professionally, from a legal, financial and business perspective," Dan replied.

He was careful with his phrasing so that Marnie didn't misinterpret the help as some type of family therapy, which he knew she felt quite capable of handling alone.

Ben was waiting for them on the deck and arose to grasp Marnie's hand and draw her in for a hug. "I think you had enough excitement for all of us last night. Tell us about the new baby."

"Well, he's just beautiful, Ben, and so healthy. I would say the mother is also doing nicely and was asking for food soon after the delivery. That's always a good sign," Marnie said. "I'll run down to see them off; the new father was telling me that, if all looks good by midday, they'll set off for their home sometime this afternoon. He said they have three other children and that they'll be excited to see the new arrival."

The fact that it was a new baby brother for three older siblings was not lost on Ben, and as the Fortunes ate, he excused himself from the table briefly. He was soon back with a sheet of paper with the names of some people for Dan and Marnie to talk with so they could start to get a grasp on their challenges.

"Dan, Marnie, this list isn't a long one. I've written down the names and contact details of three people I trust. I think together or separately they can help you," he said. "Initially, you need to give them the space to be of service to you. Tell them your story and how you feel about where you're at. No one's going to judge you. They'll listen to you for as long as it takes and you'll need to be willing to answer their questions. I can tell you that when my son Kevin came to me about continuing CDC on his own, we used these people and I'm thankful I did.

"Those insights at that time allowed me to get above the issues and extricate myself from the day to day to establish my legacy in my own mind before committing to the actual transactions and transitions that followed."

Marnie turned to Dan with a look of resolve. "This sounds like something we should do, Danny. Can we afford not to try?" Dan reached his hand across to hers, touched her and nodded.

Later that day, with Ben waving farewell from the dock and the seaplane lined up into the wind, they accelerated across the waters of the cove and leapt into the air. Marnie had the pilot give a tip of the wings to their host as they circled back over the compound and noticed the new baby with his parents being readied for the journey back to their home.

Looking down, she smiled and pressed her hand against the window until they were out of sight.

The Family Office

Higgins let out a great yawn and rolled over onto his side, one eye on his treat box, hoping Carrie Wilson would notice and give him a piece of biscuit. It was now 6:30 p.m. and the office staff had been gone for 90 minutes. The golden retriever had picked the wrong time, though, as Carrie was fully engaged in a document on her computer screen that she hoped to bring to some sort of final draft before leaving for the day.

Ever tenacious, though, the dog easily rolled to a seated position and with a steady force of his head, moved his mouth into the middle of her free hand and just paused with it there. Carrie, sensing her dog's careful intrusion, momentarily shifted her eyes from her work on the screen. She met Higgins's gaze evenly and then asked, "Is it that time already? Didn't I just give you a snack less than an hour ago?" She returned her gaze to the screen as if to tell her pet, "Not a chance."

Carrie had formerly worked in corporate law with a larger, established firm before deciding that the type of work she excelled at was better accomplished through a smaller boutique operation that catered to the needs of privately held companies and their family shareholders. Being able to create her own rules about bringing pets to work was an added bonus of going down the entrepreneurial route.

If nothing else, Higgins was the model of persistence when it came to getting his own way on two areas of his life: snacking and going out for walks. As it was late in the day and Carrie wanted to buy a little more time on her document, she gave in to the dog fairly easily and casually flipped him half a biscuit, which he caught cleanly in his mouth in mid-air.

"Now go lie down and let me finish, or better yet, earn your keep and go give Roger this mail," she said, and picked through the mail for the right envelope and placed it in Higgins's mouth. The dog, having learned this particular game as a pup, knew it meant taking the letter as proffered and bringing it to Carrie's partner, Roger Mason, down the hall. He also knew that getting the envelope there relatively slobber free was an effective way of double-ending on the biscuit, as Roger kept a box of the treats as well.

Off he went to find Roger on his headset, engaged with a client in a discussion about a tax issue that was unique to the client's family-held business structure. He gave Higgins permission to come in with a quick wave of his hand and took the envelope while reaching back for a treat. He stuffed a piece into the dog's mouth and watched their canine office assistant happily trot away, having successfully completed the biscuit ruse yet again.

Roger hadn't let his attention to the phone conversation slide for a second and asked the caller several questions about his thinking on the proposed scenario. The client explained the premise of what he wanted to accomplish, or rather what he wanted accomplished through the advice and actions of GBA which was the company name of Roger and Carrie's family office. After Roger did a quick check on the whereabouts and happenings of the client's family, the call neared its conclusion.

After they exchanged goodbyes, Roger allowed his eyes to drop to the envelope. It was distinct due to the postage stamp on it, and he knew that letters like that came from only one place and one person.

Eyebrows raised, he thought of Ben Curtis. Now what would he want, he wondered. When he heard from Ben, it was always by phone or they met in person. He didn't usually send a letter, especially at this time of year.

Roger and Carrie provided family office services to the Curtis family through GBA. In this role they managed and provided oversight of all governance matters and the integration of their legal, accounting, tax and investment requirements. They had originally met through Roger's work with Ben on the Curtis family's succession structure and the passing of the torch from Ben's generation. Ben had been involved in family succession planning as a younger man when his own father had retired, but the size and scope of what was now a Curtis land development company was more complex. Ben had thought it important to have specialized professional perspectives on the issues at hand throughout the entire process.

When they had agreed that they were a fit for each other, Ben had told him something that Roger had often relayed to others in the same circumstances as the Curtises and CDC. "Roger, we're embarking on what will become my legacy. To do this correctly, it will have to be an exceedingly well thought out legal, accounting and tax process, but to truly succeed here, we can't lose sight of it being primarily a people process. This has to work for all of us in our family as people. I've always believed that becoming successful financially and ending my life an unhappy grouch would be a stupid idea. Don't you agree?"

Roger had wordlessly nodded, pleased at Ben's early grasp on this most basic objective. He later came to realize that Ben had a wonderful way of cutting through the superfluous and identifying the critical in common terms.

"Roger, we need a structure as a family that allows us to fulfill what we value—what we value collectively as a family and then generationally as individuals." That statement jumped out whenever Roger remembered the opening conversation with Ben and his wife Ginny.

Reaching for his letter opener, Roger carefully cut the envelope and inside found only one page. It was a photocopy of a handwritten list of contact information that included Carrie and himself along with a colleague they often worked with, Tom Coyle.

Fortune's Impasse

There on a sticky pad note was a note in Ben's familiar scrawl.

> Roger: I trust you are well and the rest of the office, too. I have given the original of this contact page to dear friends of mine, Dan and Marnie Fortune. It will serve as an introduction to you and your team as well as your contact details. I have recommended that Mr. and Mrs. Fortune contact you directly. I do hope you can meet when convenient as it would be a very apt and appropriate place for him to start with a problem that their family is grappling with. I will leave it to him to fill you in on the nature of his problem and to you to listen carefully in turn!
>
> Regards, Ben

Roger stared at Ben's note for another few seconds, trying to recall where he'd heard the name Fortune before. Just then, Carrie drifted by the door, headed for the server room which was the boutique office's technology hub. With the confidential documents of several families and their business requirements coming through the office as e-files or needing to be scanned, they had a surprising amount of storage requirements for each client.

"Carrie, this letter from Ben Curtis, did it arrive today in the mail?" he called out down the hall. Carrie retraced her steps and stood at the doorway. "Yes, it did. I haven't looked through everything, but I did recognize the postage on that envelope and knew you'd like to see it. What's it all about?"

"Well, he's introduced us to a family that are personal friends. Does the name *Fortune* ring a bell with you?" he asked.

"Not sure on that."

"It should sound familiar to me, but I can't put a finger on it," Roger said. "Anyway, it'll come to me. How are you coming with that land transfer structure you're working on? Remember we have to have some type of strategy when we meet next week with the Todds. Are you stuck?"

"No," Carrie said, "but I do have to double-check a few things in several jurisdictions before I feel comfortable advising them to move forward with their plans. They just can't—. Hang on. I know that name, *Fortune*. Doesn't the F in FCI mean Fortune? Fortune Consolidated Industries?"

Typing FCI into the search engine on his computer, Roger said, "Yes. Interesting ... all those retail grocery operations in CDC developments are FCI's. That must be the link back to Ben Curtis."

"What do you suppose the issue is?" Carrie wondered.

Roger leaned back in his desk chair. "Well, I suppose they face many of the same challenges that everyone with that kind of success face. How do we cede control of our business as we age in a way that's appropriate, and can we maximize our valuation for the benefit of ourselves and the next generations?"

Roger shook his head as if to clear the assumptions that it was easy to make with potential clients not yet met. "But you know what? I imagine we'll hear from this gentleman soon enough, and every situation is unique so it will be important that we be a proper sounding board."

Losing Sleep

Dan Fortune sat in his car, reviewing some messages on his smartphone. The parking facility attached to the GBA offices was rapidly emptying as people headed home for the day.

He was waiting for Marnie to join him for the meeting with the people at GBA. She had called and left a message that she would be a little late. Dan's first reaction was that she wasn't taking the meeting seriously enough, but quickly realized that they were both deeply committed to it.

For Dan, calling to arrange the meeting had been a tough phone call to make. He wondered if he couldn't just apply a little more force to the situation to make everything work out on its own. Sharing all this with an outsider was not something Dan relished, but he did trust the judgment of one person more than anyone else he'd met in business and that was Ben Curtis. If Ben said these were the people he should deal with, then he would do that.

When they had arrived back from Ben's, he had been immediately pulled back into the feud between Fanny and Jeff. He could sense that throughout the management team there was lost momentum at FCI, as people had started taking sides, trying to guess who might win and be left standing at the end of it all.

Win? Dan mused. There will be no winning anything for anybody if this isn't brought under control and quickly. They were already losing momentum on critical issues affecting FCI, and it peeved Dan that what was essentially an internal people issue would soon affect FCI's products and ultimately its customers.

The only news Dan could feel good about was that Jimmy's situation appeared to be stabilizing. The night Jeff and Dan had gone to the police station had been tough on all of them. Jimmy was released to his family. The media furor after the arrest was made public had not been as damaging as Dan had feared. Jimmy's role had been distilled down in the press reports to him being a "found-in." Though Dan and Marnie struggled with not doing anything, they had decided to let the investigation reach its conclusion.

Officer Mike Simons had called a few days afterwards to share the news with Jeff that Jimmy would not be charged. "Jeff, Jimmy's a first-time offender and there's no reason to run him through the system at this point. In this case, he has made some bad decisions and chosen some bad associations. But—" Simons paused to make sure Jeff heard his point in the correct context, "everyone makes mistakes at some point.

"Do us a favor and tell your family to keep close to him. I've seen this before and it looks more like a case of boredom and lack of purpose than anything criminal. Your brother is a thoughtful young man. There's nothing as vulnerable as a young guy trying to find his way forward in life," the officer continued.

"I think we both know that the criminal system doesn't need a Jimmy Fortune to deal with when there are bigger problems out there. Besides, what most people need in these situations is a strong family. You and your family have to give yourselves a chance to sort this out. I would compare it to you having a basket of dirty laundry that you want to hand off to me. The best thing I can do is hand the basket back to you and remind you that you can and should be doing this laundry yourself.

"We have so few cases of this type where those that mess up come from solid family backgrounds. I'm not saying *never*, mind you, but it is seldom. Family is the best vehicle to pass on shared values in society. From what I know of you and Jen, it appears you both were raised right. I'd be surprised if Jimmy couldn't get moving in the right direction if everyone put in a concerted effort to keep him accountable to himself and to all of you."

"Mike, I can't thank you enough and I think you're right. Certainly Jimmy needs to man up on this one and reach his own potential. But we've let him down by not keeping the connection as tight as we could have. As Jimmy's only brother, I can tell you that growing up in our family wasn't all it looks like to an outsider. Our father is a driven man. I don't think he would have attained the level of success he has without aggressiveness. He gets his way in business because of that.

"My sisters and I grew up knowing our parents loved us and, because we were close in age, we had the rivalries that any siblings have. Our father was gone all the time. He let our mother call the shots on most things and we endured." Jeff took a breath as he realized he was in unknown terrain, discussing his personal thoughts with his friend.

"When I say we endured, Mike, it may sound strange to you. Yes, it was a life of privilege and enduring it doesn't sound that hard, but we were swept up in the build-out of FCI. Every time we became stable as a family, another opportunity for growth came along. From an early age, the three of us came to understand that this was our burden as a family and it somehow solidified things for us. We had all experienced those lean years together. Cash was tight for us," Jeff said.

"My father took a huge gamble and struggled to make those payments on the obligations he'd signed onto. Heck, there's home movie footage of me when I was four, saying all I wanted to get for Christmas was two cans of tuna and some mini-cars." His voice broke a bit as he struggled, not knowing whether to laugh or cry. "My father told me once that being on the other side of that camera and hearing me say that was heartrending for him, knowing how close the extremes of success and oblivion were at that point.

"Jimmy's quite a bit younger than the rest of us. He's 12 years younger than I am and 11 years younger than Inge. He grew up alone and from where I sit, was left on his own as my parents started to enjoy their lives as older adults. They certainly made sure Jimmy didn't lack anything, but he was always given money instead of time. It was awkward because I think everyone knew this wasn't the way it had been in our youth, but it evolved over time."

Mike was right. He decided they would all have to re-engage with Jimmy over the next while and bring him into the fold, one way or another. Jeff thanked his friend again and they hung up. He thought about the discussion for a few minutes after making a note to cover it that evening with Jen and see what she thought a solution might look like. He went back to his desk and started to review his email, not bothering to read the ones Fanny was sending to the FCI management team. It all just felt to him like a waste of his time and he felt personally derailed. He decided he would focus on his area of FCI for now.

Dan sat there after explaining things to Roger and Carrie, as Marnie looked on. "I feel a bit cornered here on these issues. It's causing me a great deal of stress. I'm back to not sleeping right. I haven't felt this way in almost 50 years—out of control and unsure of where I'm headed, like I've lost my bearings on my destination. I'm in a situation that I've tried to avoid my entire adult life. I don't have an answer and it scares the hell out of me."

Other than a few clarifying questions, Roger and Carrie sat quietly and listened to Dan and Marnie share their story from their respective positions. Their points of view varied in some areas and in others were remarkably aligned.

When debriefing by themselves afterward, Roger and Carrie would both feel there were some obvious points that would need to be addressed, but also that, fundamentally, there was much that was sound in what the Fortunes disclosed.

Roger wanted to make certain he understood how the Fortunes felt and asked Dan to clarify a few areas. "You feel cornered? How so? What does that feel like to both of you? Marnie, are you in agreement? Is that how you feel?"

They both nodded, letting the questions resonate for a while. Then Marnie, raising herself in her chair and looking out the window to the streetscape, started to speak. "Now, Dan, this will be hard for you to hear but I just feel it's time for us to step back from this and think about whether you need to be involved in FCI anymore. There are things we should be doing now. If we don't, we'll regret it one day.

"That day is closer than either of us wants to admit, but it will come. It came for your father, Dan, and it came for my mother. I can't handle the idea of you going out with your boots on like your father or me getting stricken with something like my mother and knowing we didn't do a thing to help ourselves.

"With mother dying so young, she didn't get much of a chance at things. My father raised my sisters and me by himself and we couldn't have had a better life. My regret, though, is that he gave himself to us. While he never would have admitted it, he denied himself opportunities—for expanding his practice, taking on more teaching opportunities at the university, even finding another woman to share his life with. He always said he did what he had to do, but I realize now that with what you and I have built, Dan, it makes it all a little hollow if we never answer the question, what's it all for?"

Dan cut into the conversation with some outward impatience. "Marnie, have you thought about what it would mean to the company if I stepped aside right now? FCI is at a crossroads. Fanny and Jeff are fighting like cats and dogs; the rest of the management team is standing by, watching all of this shake out."

Dan stared past all at the table. "I think they're starting to doubt our family has what it takes to keep this rolling. In the business section, there are rumours of FCI's issues, and some columnists are wondering if we're in play and looking for a buyout. I can tell you it breaks my heart. Mark my words: right now there are at least a few and maybe more key FCI people getting calls from recruiters in the industry, asking if they'd consider moving to other situations.

"Granted, we still need a few pieces and to see if everyone sees FCI in a similar way, but I've busted my ass assembling a good core group. They'll leave if there's a hint that something isn't right. People have a problem with instability. Not everyone's an entrepreneur and any sniff they get of their employment being at risk will cause them to vote with their feet and leave us."

Marnie tried reason. "We have a chance to enjoy what we've built and the time we have left," she said. "But the help we need has to be as much about our personal circumstances as the concerns of FCI. And then we also need to consider the children. This thing with Jimmy has brought it home for me that loss of purpose is dangerous and can make people feel unwell and not worthy," Marnie said. "I don't like looking at what this has the potential of becoming. I think we're at a make-or-break point here."

Dan shook his head in bewilderment. "I just don't know what to do other than what I've always done."

He turned to Roger, who'd been taking in the conversation with interest but with an emotional detachment. He knew that what this couple needed at this point was to be listened to above all.

"What can you do for me? Are we sunk?" Dan asked in exasperation, with a nervous laugh.

Roger let the question hang for a few moments to reflect on what he and Carrie had been told. In his experience, Roger had come to understand that, in emotionally charged circumstances, it was easy to slip into the clients' angst; however, this emerging sympathy was of no value to the client in getting to an ideal outcome. If you aren't part of the solution then you're just another part of the problem, he often reminded himself and others working on projects like these. An empathic mindset kept one above the fray.

Instead, it was important to stay slightly above the fray, he reminded himself, and keep focused on how Dan and Marnie explained the way they saw things. No, he thought, in order for us to be a solution, we have to hear this situation out completely and fully understand the perspectives of both.

"Mr. and Mrs. Fortune, I want to start to answer that question by thanking you for what you've shared here tonight. These are hard subjects to talk about and I appreciate your feeling comfortable enough to talk freely.

"I'm actually going to suggest we all call it a day," he said, shifting his eyes toward Dan momentarily to see him flinch at the delay, which he knew was a physical sign of stress and his sense of urgency, betraying his desire to get an immediate solution underway.

"I can say that your situation is one we've seen before. One of the areas of our practice is the methodology that surrounds family-held business succession. We need to meet again soon, and we can lay out a framework to develop a shared understanding of the situation. From that shared understanding, we'll guide you through a process that will permit you to find your own path forward. I believe this situation can be rectified, and perhaps significant value can be added to all concerned, not only in FCI's valuation, but in the extended Fortune family and of course for both of you as principal founders.

"Frankly, though, I think we should all sleep on what you have said. Believe me when I say we can help, but the value of that help will be greatly magnified by what we do when we next meet. Carrie and I will introduce you to a very simple model that will allow you to identify for yourselves where you feel you're at, where you should go and what needs to be addressed. By not moving forward this evening, we put some distance between the problem and its potential solutions. Putting some space between a question and its answer is often the first step to clarity and a resolution," Roger pointed out.

"Your resolve will be an important component to moving this forward from problem to opportunity. Committing to a process like succession requires decisions that are made with a clear mind and forethought. What matters is getting it right on every level," Roger said.

"Yes, we know. Ben told us. It is legal, tax and accounting processes all together but has to be centered on the needs of people, was how he put it," Marnie said, starting to warm to the project and seeing the wisdom of the temporary delay Roger had suggested.

"What's your time like tomorrow late day?" Roger asked.

"Why don't we start at the same time as we did tonight?" said Carrie. "I can call Tom Coyle and see if he can sit in. Tom's a member of our succession team as well and will have his own questions for you on this process. Is that okay with you both?"

After they decided on a time, the Fortunes took the elevator down to the car park. The dealership concierge had arranged to pick up Marnie's car for servicing right from the garage, allowing her to travel back home with Dan, which gave them a chance to talk.

They were halfway back home before Dan spoke. Looking over at his wife he said quietly, "Well, I guess it's time to start sorting things out, isn't it? It's just so hard to do."

"Dan, I trust Ben's judgment, and he told us these people were the best. I feel we've been listened to this evening and I've appreciated it. My father always said Rome wasn't built in a day. I don't think you can expect them to have instantaneous answers.

"This situation has evolved over a long time, but we can do it. We just have to get everybody on the same page. I would have been worried if Roger had hurried us. As a matter of fact, I wouldn't have felt comfortable. I like them and I'm pleased we're moving forward."

When they arrived home, there were no signs of life in the house, but the garage doors were open with the light streaming out into the darkness. They saw Jimmy bent over a classic car that Dan had kept over the years, and they could see he was deeply engaged in applying a coat of wax.

Dan and Marnie exchanged glances as he brought the car to a halt outside the garage and stepped out.

"Hey, what's up, Jim?" Dan asked, slightly bemused by his son's activity.

"Well, I've been doing some thinking, Dad. It's time I started doing something around here when I can. I was hoping to surprise you by shining up your Shelby," Jimmy said as he finished buffing the last panel on the car.

"Well, you sure have done a wonderful job, Jim. I've wanted to get around to it myself." One of the things Dan enjoyed most about being with his son as he was growing up was working on the Shelby together when Dan could find the time. Jimmy's gesture brought him back to those days for a moment.

"Well, I know I have caused you some problems lately and I just want to put it all behind us," Jimmy said, looking directly up at Dan. "When I saw you coming down that hall behind Jeff at the lockup, I knew you were feeling pretty terrible and that it was totally my fault. I realize I can't let you and Mom down like that ever again. I don't know yet what I can do with my life, but I do know I have to do whatever it is and take charge of my future now."

Watching from the doorway inside, Marnie briefly welled up with pride in her son and then said, "Let's see what we can find in here for dinner for the three of us," and turned down the hallway toward the kitchen, realizing she'd just witnessed a small victory.

Just Between Us

The next day, Roger stood at his office window looking down over the city traffic, tapping the glass with his finger as he worked through what he'd heard from Dan and Marnie the previous evening. He started to visualize what the follow-up conversation would look like, based on previous experience with families like the Fortunes.

He thought back to the look on their faces and the quick glances they'd exchanged when he said that embarking on succession was in itself a multidimensional experience. It took in various professions and contributions of tested concepts that needed to meld into one overall plan. It could be complex if the outcomes were to be good for all involved.

Roger knew that failing to adequately plan and then effectively implement a succession plan was one of the major destroyers of wealth, especially where a family business was involved. Intergenerational succession was a hurdle that every successful family enterprise faced eventually. He knew that a myriad of emotions would come out of the discussions ahead.

Roger felt that the core team members were quite capable of listening well. This focus required the understanding of each participant's perspective. However, the moment they crossed the invisible line and lapsed into feeling as the clients felt, the value of the external advisory team eroded, if not disappeared entirely.

He always felt that, at this point, no matter who clients were and what their situation was, the crux of the challenge for everybody would be simply how to get it all underway, starting with that opening discussion.

There was a damp cold front coming into the area. It was a late fall day that, depending on where the wind blew from, could turn to winter in an hour or two. With just enough moisture on the inside of the window, he could doodle a bit with his finger, and he started to draw a diagram.

The sketched drawing was an idea he used often with people like the Fortunes. It would be their hand on the pencil and their own insight into how they saw the family business circumstances that would initiate positive change in the picture created. Once the picture was complete, they could see at a glance where they were already secure as well as those areas where the overall family enterprise was vulnerable.

He stood back to contemplate the picture, when Carrie popped her head through the doorway and said, "Higgins has to get out of the office for a bit so I'm going to be out. I'll grab you a green tea as well."

She saw that Roger had been absentmindedly doodling on the window. "Oh yeah, that's going to make the cleaners happy," she admonished her partner. "How about we keep our creativity on the whiteboard?"

"Yeah, I shouldn't do that. I was just imagining the Fortune situation. What time are they in here, 4 pm?" he asked.

With an abrupt bark, Higgins alerted Carrie that there was some urgency to their outing and she turned and called over her shoulder, "Yes, 4:00 sharp." He returned his gaze to the window.

When Marnie and Dan arrived, they were greeted by Nikki Kingsmill, GBA's office manager, who took their coats and quickly ushered the couple into the meeting room. It was purposely not set up boardroom style; instead, a large round table dominated the space. The circular table was purposely chosen for GBA so that no one sat in a position of superiority as it often was with a traditional rectangular set-up. Everyone at these meetings was expected to be an equal contributor and listener.

Already seated was a man who was looking away from the entryway, immersed in writing something on his notepad. As the Fortunes took in their surroundings, the fellow got up to greet them with a handshake and introduce himself. "I'm Tom Coyle and you must be the Fortunes."

Marnie and Dan nodded, allowing Tom to continue. "I work with Roger and Carrie on certain clients where they feel I can add value to the initial discussion. They gave me a call and I was able to come by. I hope it's okay with you?"

Dan, sensing he should take the lead, said, "Yes, Tom. Carrie had mentioned that you'd be coming in and might be able to add something to our conversation. We appreciate that you were able to join in. Now tell me, Tom, before Roger and Carrie get in here and just between us, what exactly is going to happen?"

"Well, that's going to depend, but can I ask you a question or two before I comment on that?" Tom replied, noticing Dan furrowing his brow at the delay on finding out his answer. "Your opening meeting, I understand it, was last evening. How did you feel it went? Were you listened to?"

Marnie spoke up now, nodding in agreement. "Actually, I felt really good about it and, after one of the best night's sleep I've had in a long time, I feel even more positive today."

Dan countered his wife's gusto subtly. "Well, I didn't sleep as well as she did, but I guess I did feel listened to. That was all great, but my concern is still how all this stuff is going to affect everything I've done up till now. We're a solid company. There's nothing so terrible that focus and sticking to our path won't solve."

Tom recognized Dan's mindset as one that was common amongst entrepreneurs, that a little more push would solve most problems, and he didn't disagree. "Dan there are a lot of great businesses out there, but the most important one is your own. This is a health checkup of sorts. We are going to make sure you both get clarity on how you see the bigger picture and ascertain all your options.

"Of course, I'm certainly aware of FCI. My wife and I are in one of your stores at least weekly. Her parents were loyal customers before that, throughout her childhood.

"I guess I always liked those radio commercials you ran back eight or ten years ago, where the guy talked about how his family was in business to help other families, and that slogan at the end of each one, 'Simple family fare from simpler times.' They were great. Very memorable," Tom said.

"Whatever happened to that guy that did the voiceover on those? I wonder what he's doing," Tom mused, wrapped up in his own reflection and not noticing the surprised chuckles coming from the couple.

"Well, would you believe those ran for a span of eighteen years but were first on air almost thirty years ago? Those were my favorites," Marnie recalled, her eyes brimming with tears.

"And that guy you have clearly consigned to the 'Where are they now' file, well that was me," Dan growled through a slight smile, clearly loving that Tom had somehow been left with that fragment of brand recognition after all those years. "Those spots haven't run in any market in this century, but I do thank you for remembering."

At that point, Roger and Carrie came in to the meeting, greeted everyone and took their seats. Turning to the Fortunes, Carrie noticed that Nikki had provided a jug of water for the table and that all present had a fresh cup of tea or coffee poured. Carrie said, "Well, looks like we're set and we're all here. Let's begin."

No one noticed that Higgins had pushed through the door, as well, before Nikki closed it. He took his usual place on the rug by the window with a quiet sigh, settling down for a rest, happy to get some respite from the duties of being an office dog.

Roger led off. "Folks, at this point we need to get into the opening stage of a solution for you. This solution needs to work not only for you but also for FCI and the next Fortune generations. I'm sure you're in agreement on that. Now there will obviously be others involved, but at this point as you're both in total control of things, it's important that we validate how you see things first. In the days ahead, we'll start to bring in members of the second generation as well as those non-related professional managers that work at FCI.

"Let's start this discussion with an ideal end or outcome in mind. In essence, it's harder to start than it is to end so we will start with the end in mind.

"All of us involved; whether it's you and Marnie, your family members, your non-related professional managers at FCI or outside professionals like us that figure into your succession, we need to be in sync and working toward an understood ideal outcome.

"Well, Dan, I'm sure you've heard of Yogi Berra, the old baseball player and pontificator of simple truths. He said something like 'If you don't know where you are going, you'll end up someplace else.'"

Dan suppressed a smile. He'd heard the Yogi saying long ago or had perhaps read it on the sports page. He'd always believed it to be true. Having a clear objective in mind with a point of view that was teachable to others was the way to achieve desired outcomes.

Roger continued, "From what I've seen, there are a lot more people that fail to plan than there are those who actively plan to fail. Yet failure can be an unforeseen result. I think we can all agree that without a well thought out intention, planning is ineffectual in achieving 'good' results.

"One of the reasons you both are where you are is your pragmatic optimism. It has seen you through when things got a bit dark. There are better days ahead. You both know that. So let's use back-to-the-result thinking."

Turning back to the rest of the group, he said, "So the basic question woven through all this is always, What does 'good' look like?"

He gave them some time to jot down some notes on paper and collect their thoughts.

Marnie was first to jump in. "I want happiness and peace of mind for all of us in the family. I want my children and their children to experience for themselves what it feels like to have wins that they created themselves and to experience self-reliance. It's important that they feel successful and not just that they're living the results of success. I'd like to be able to give back to society. We've been blessed. We should share and make our positive mark on the universe. Finally, I want the winter of our lives to be what's right for us as a couple. I want Dan to be able to have the time to restore that biplane he bought and enjoy his car collection."

"What do you want for yourself, Marnie?" Tom asked. "All your outcomes are about other people."

"Are they?" Marnie replied a little self-consciously. Quietly, even shyly, she added, "Perhaps I might like to go back to school. There are so many things I'm interested in that I have left to learn. My perfect day is in a library."

"Thanks, Marnie. Those points are a great start," Roger said. "How about you, Dan? What did you come up with?"

"Well, mine are mostly my concerns for FCI. And I have a few," Dan said, pushing the bridge of his glasses slightly further up his nose. "First, I want to clearly understand what all my options are for FCI. Do I sell out? Do I look at a management buyout? I've heard of some people like me who retain control but bring in a hired gun to run their shop, and if that person is good maybe give up a little piece. Would the staff be interested in buying in through an employee share ownership plan?"

Dan's mind raced and his words fell on top of each other as he spilled out where he was at on outcomes. "I probably should think of ways of involving my children, at least the two that seem to be interested. Although granted, I'm not that happy with what's going on between them lately. I'd like to get Jimmy involved in some way. I don't think Inge will ever come around, and perhaps it's not her path.

"At the end of the day, I'd hate to see the choice we make impinge on FCI's valuation. That company, *my* company—" and then catching Marnie's raised eyebrows "—I mean *our* company, is a family legacy and it doesn't have to die. People will always need food, won't they? Why can't I—we, I mean, it—live forever?" He looked up and made eye contact with everyone at the table, glad he'd stated his true feelings.

Sensing that the tenor of the conversation needed to change in order to allow Dan to collect himself, Tom interrupted the flow with a suggestion. "Let's take a breather here and come back in 10 minutes and continue. Roger, Carrie, when we come back, I think it makes sense to show the Fortunes a bit about the model the three of us use and how it evolved. Is everyone up for that?"

Marnie and Dan were glad to be able to stop for a while. Dan went to the window for a look across the city, and Marnie excused herself to check her messages.

F³®[1]—What Does "Good" Look Like?

When they all returned, Carrie was at the front of the room next to the whiteboard.

Marnie had now settled back in her chair, ready to get to work. Dan stayed forward, both hands on the table clasped, his body language still a bit tentative.

Turning to the Fortunes, Carrie said, "I think you'll find our F³® model is a good way to think through the issues surrounding your next step and, in the end, will help bring you the collective awareness needed to tackle a succession plan.

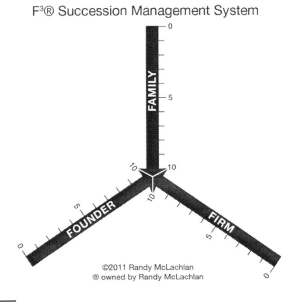

---

[1] F³ is a registered trademark of Randy McLachlan

"We find this a simple yet effective way to illustrate a concept. More accurately, it's a good way for our clients to explain their unique situation to us and to each other," she explained. She turned toward the whiteboard and started to sketch out a drawing that had three arms coming into a central point. Each of the arms had a gradient scale of 0 to 10 and was the same length. Marnie noted that with Carrie's flair, she seemed to be implying depth. The drawing, when completed, had a draftsman's geometric dimensionality to it.

Carrie continued, "Now each of these arms describes one of the key factors involved in every transition plan we see with privately held companies like yours. When completed and combined, the mapping of these 3 arms reflect the interrelationship of these factors from the perspective of each person or group doing the assessment."

"Why did you call it an F^3, Carrie?" Marnie asked.

"These three axes represent the coming together of the three key perspectives that most influence success in the transition of a privately held company: *Founder*, *Family* and *Firm*. Thus, F^3."

"What I've tried to illustrate here is a way for each of the key players to express his or her view of the world at a point in time. By sharing each perspective with the other key players, they can collectively assess the level of alignment amongst their various interests and goals. They may also use this model and process to identify where the root issues and greatest opportunities for improvement exist."

"So how does it work, then?" asked Dan. "Are the arms a reflection of how the company looks to me? I don't think it's as neat and tidy as that."

Before Carrie had a chance to reply, Marnie responded to Dan, slowly shaking her head. "No, honey. I think this is maybe a representation of how we perceive things, but can we let this lady continue?" Marnie recognized Dan's impatient approach to getting to the end.

Carrie took the opportunity to move further into her explanation of the model. "The gradient on the arms is from 0 to 10, with 10 being perfection and 0 quite imperfect. The scale moves from 0 at the outer edge toward the point of intersection that you could think of as 10. As I said, we'll help you use this tool for your own situation later, but consider this an example for now.

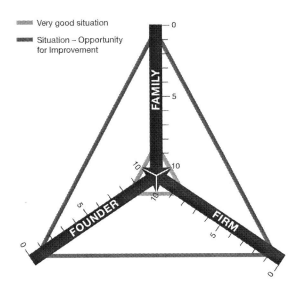

"The model's value is in our client being able to identify the big picture individually and from the perspective of all parties to the process. The *Founder* arm should reflect how independent of the business the founder feels, both financially and emotionally, Dan," Carrie said.

Dan, watching carefully now, shifted further into his chair, finally giving the upholstered seatback a reason to be there.

"Okay, yes, I'm with you so far," he allowed, looking over the tops of his eyeglasses at Carrie.

"So in one way, what's important to understand is where the founder identifies his or her financial dependence or independence on what the firm can provide as month-to-month personal cash flow for the founder or founders. Some are financially independent of their business and don't require the paycheck any longer. They would have other sources of investment income. There are others, though, depending on their burn rate and lifestyle demands, who might require that draw on a monthly basis."

Roger joined in to Carrie's explanation, empathetically adding, "I can say this. Experience has taught me that there are two fundamental types of dependency where a private family business is involved. The first is a financial dependence on the business. The second is an emotional dependence on the business.

"This part of the process is focused on probing and understanding the extent of your financial dependence on FCI. Some founders require every cent from the business. What's most common, though, after looking at their financial needs during the process, is for founders to place themselves somewhere in between best case and worst case. Most important is to be honest and accurate in the self-assessment, as the other arms demand this accuracy for the best overall plan."

Reassuring the Fortunes, Roger said, "This is a confidential area for our clients. However, it's important to get a true picture. Our happiest clients have told us that this exercise alone is"—he chose his next words carefully—"strangely liberating and empowering. The ensuing clarity is a linchpin in connecting all the other arms."

There was a pause as Marnie and Dan digested what they had seen to that point. Dan, thinking of Jimmy's night in the lockup, could visualize the analogy.

Roger continued. "A founder's emotional dependence on the business at a personal, community and social level is also an area for honest self-assessment. This is often the most significant barrier to an effective transition. Here's an example of a situation where a founder's attachment to the business was a defining part of her psyche. She had worked hard as part of her transition plan to develop other areas through which she could make a meaningful contribution and make the focus of her energy, skills and emotion. By doing this, she gave herself, her family and her business the great gift of flexibility. She was in the position to redefine her role to fit with the needs and expectations of the business and her family, if the ultimate decision was to keep the business in the family. On the other hand, she was prepared to step out entirely if the business was sold, without leaving a gaping hole in her life.

"This emotional attachment issue also needs to be looked at from the perspective of the business. Is the firm exclusively identified with the founder or has it developed its own community position over the years? Some marketing experts refer to that as the *corporate brand* and they're right, though purely at a market level. However, what a founder should also be concerned with is the company's ability to stand on its own without him or her. We'll dig into that again and many other considerations in the *Firm* arm of the model," Roger said, finishing his input for the moment.

Carrie took over again, saying, "The *Family* arm is where the client assesses the affinity his or her family has for the business and each other. Some of the thought here is around whether there's an opportunity for the next generation to be involved. Often at least one can be either working in or looking to work in the family firm. Has a natural fit for the business developed in any of the next generation? Are there members of the next generation who are set in other careers? A deep dive on this arm will help all of us assess whether keeping FCI in the family into the next generation is a good fit with where the next generation sees itself going and, if so, what can be done to make that as good a fit as possible.

"This may be a particularly sensitive question," Carrie continued. "Is there an unhealthy competitiveness in the family that diminishes a sibling in any way? Occasionally the family firm is viewed with apathy, or an attitude of intentional disengagement is apparent."

Marnie now nodded slowly as she took in the direction and intent of the *Family* arm in the F³ model. Looking at Dan and then back to the others, she said, "I'm pretty sure my husband's and my own perspective on that piece differs, let alone where the rest of the family stands and what they'll say. How can these gaps be bridged?" she added gloomily.

"Every family is different, Marnie," Roger replied as he poured a glass of water from the pitcher. "Remember, we're talking about the use of the model and not necessarily your own family.

"We'll go through this in detail when you invite your family members into this discussion. Depending on who's involved, there will always be some unique considerations that come into play with the *Family* arm."

Carrie, finished with her overview on the *Family* arm, came back to the table and sat down.

Dan had been silent through the last few minutes as family was discussed. "What are my options going to be within my family? That's what I need to know. FCI needs somebody to be in charge. It will slowly strangle itself if no one can step up."

"Dan, the third arm is where we get into the business side or what we will call the *Firm*," Roger said. "I believe it makes sense for Tom here to take you through this piece in explaining our model."

"Thank you, Roger," said Tom. "In succession situations where there's an active operating company that's still privately held within the family and controlled by the founders, it's important to address and acknowledge the firm as an equal and independent party. Dan, Marnie, the piece that has made all this possible is of course FCI. Part of our process on the road ahead is to spend some time with who you consider to be the main stakeholders in the FCI of the present.

"We'll gather FCI's thought leaders, its forward thinkers, those active family members in your business, as well as members of the executive team and of course yourselves. What we cover in this area is another dimension. Obviously part of it has a lot to do with the founders, but now focuses on the founder in relation to the operating company."

"What if the founder really likes being involved," Dan said, chortling. "What if, try as they might, the executive team can't get rid of him?"

There was a brief pause as Tom took in Dan's comment. "Well, within this arm of the process, there's ample opportunity for those people to fill in the founder on that," he answered with a chuckle.

After fully registering the comment and follow-up question, Tom more seriously added, "Dan, you might be underestimating yourself, but we can and will cover that piece further in the process."

It was common, he knew, for founders to have an inaccurate picture of just what his or her intrinsic value was when succession happened within a mature company. There was great value to the firm if the founder wasn't selling outright and wanted to stay partially involved with an emeritus status. There was an opportunity there to be viewed as a bastion of sober second thought when situations occurred outside the norm and senior leadership wanted a founder's involvement.

Most founders felt either that they needed to be too involved or that they should be totally out of the picture. Tom had seen that each succession was different. The degree of involvement needed to be handled with sensitivity and respect. He knew that this arm, just like the two others, was a sensitive area for most founders. The loss of control had the potential to cause an agonizing point in time when the founder has to come to terms with his or her own mortality.

It was a tough one, Tom knew, and covering it in sync with the other elements of the F^3 process was the best way to help a founder get through the decision. This process would help untangle the mess of issues that get all wrapped together in normal course. Aspects such as the founder's financial and emotional independence from the firm, treating the family fairly when the bulk of the assets are tied up in the firm, children who've already invested heavily in or become dependent on the firm, children who want to be the next leaders but are not ready and may never be, children who aren't interested in the firm as a legacy asset, and so on, all converge to put strain on the survival of their "first child."

Pointing toward his colleague, Tom continued. "Roger mentioned previously, when the *Founders* arm was covered, that it's important to assess where the business stands without its founder in the day-to-day picture. An appraisal of a firm's resiliency and its degree of independence from the founder rests on the following: Are all its customer, supplier and industry relationships operating within the shadow of the founder's oversight and involvement, or have those relationships been successfully migrated to others?

"Also important to address is the financial stability of the firm from all angles. Are there protocols and processes in place to secure the financial future of the business and its ability to meet the needs and expectations of its shareholders?"

Tom concluded his comments. "Again, it's an assessment of the firm's ability to stand alone and apart from the founder. There's a rather trifling expression, 'If you were hit by a bus…' that asks what the family or business would look like without you. I've never liked it, as it's a bit dramatic, but the point is true." He took a drink. "And that, folks, is the focus of the *Firm* arm of the F^3 model."

"Did you follow all this, Marnie?" Dan asked, giving the floor to his wife so he could save the last comment for himself.

"It looks workable and covers the areas I think are important. I especially like the equal importance it gives to addressing family," she said. "When can we get started?"

Roger had been watching Dan throughout his exposure to the F^3 model. "Dan, what are your feelings on this?"

Dan rotated his chair toward the wall and away from the others, taking a deep breath in, his eyes cast downwards and slightly to the right. He paused for a long while, as if searching for how he really felt. It was a defining moment, he knew. This F^3 model was a sound structure, he thought, and it did cover the basis of what would need to be investigated. It all sounded like some sort of archeological dig, and he wondered about the emotions of everyone involved. Did they have the tenacity that he knew this would take? Did *he*?

He closed his eyes, recalling the days of the original market location. How he had walked around after taking it over from his deceased father, his heart in his throat as he assessed what needed to be done to the building. He thought about his family's lack of money to fund any capital expenditure other than the bare minimum and about the debt that hung over his head, with a bandit like Ashley Press holding the hammer.

Dan swallowed hard now as he recalled overcoming the challenge of winning back the local shoppers to the Market and finally the kindness of Mr. Davis, and later Ben, in seeing him for what he had the potential to be.

He started to reply to Roger's question on how he felt from that position and then paused again and slowly turned his chair back to the room, facing the rest while catching Marnie's eye, just nodding his head. And then he said quietly, "Let's get this underway then."

The Founders

The planning had now started in earnest, and the Fortunes had been invited back to the meeting room a few days later to get things underway. Today the participation of Dan and Marnie was required in their capacity as founders. Roger and Carrie would lead the discussion. Tom Coyle was away, working with another client's firm.

Marnie had arrived and, as was becoming usual for her, was outwardly content and ready to contribute to the discussion. Dan had slid into the room just as the meeting started. He and Marnie had come separately today as this was a daytime meeting, commencing at mid-morning.

Dan had requested the later start. It had been ingrained in him for many years to be at his office reasonably early to go over with Tibbs the previous day's revenue picture. There was, as yet, no decision on who would be doing that. So he figured for him, anyway, it was business as usual. He poured himself a coffee, acknowledged Roger with a wave, and sat down.

Roger nodded, and everyone settled into utilizing the F^3 model to assist the Fortunes. "Dan, you and Marnie have worked hard to build FCI, and from what you've told us so far, I would think it has gotten exceedingly more complex since those days when you started out.

"As we noted the other day with the F^3 model, the idea going forward is to cut through that complexity as you try to plan out what will happen with FCI when you're no longer in the picture. Over the decades, we've used a process that has proven to help pave the road to allow for a smooth succession. This process has effectively guided business founders, their families, firms and advisors toward their optimal objective for many years."

Roger went to the whiteboard and drew a line widthwise with a few vertical lines as gradients. Underneath, he wrote "Founder Independence."

"The discussion today is about just how dependent you are, as a couple, on the business. Together, we'll explore that question with you from both a financial and nonfinancial perspective."

Roger went on to explain that, in a perfect world, following the independent assessment, the three parties—each of the founders, the family and finally the unrelated managers of the firm—would integrate the results and systematically reveal a shared view of what "good" looks like.

"However, it's not a perfect world," he cautioned. "It happens very rarely that interests and objectives naturally align. To bridge the gaps in alignment, we must use a variety of strategies, ideas and technical solutions.

"So, Marnie and Dan, in order to answer these questions effectively, we need to see where you are currently aligned as far as lifestyle, goals and objectives are concerned." Roger could see that Marnie had something to say and gave her the floor.

"How come we weren't asked to bring our family members today or even FCI people? Shouldn't they be involved in what we're doing?"

"That's a good question, Marnie," Roger replied. "We must approach that thinking from the distinct perspectives of the parties that are likely to be most affected by the succession. You're correct. Assembling others affected by all this is important. We'll get to those groups in due time, but for now we're going to stay mostly in the first area, which focuses on you and Dan as founders and your view of the world.

"There will be time for the input and perspective of others. When we get to those others, it will be very valuable to the overall process. However, we need you to be a little selfish today and only consider yourselves."

At this, Marnie nodded, accepting the logic. She struggled inwardly though. It was against her nature to not be thinking inclusively, particularly where family was involved. However, she knew that for Dan it was vital that they tackle the ideas one step at a time and help take him logically to what would, in the end, be quite an emotional step.

"The first area of independence we'll cover with you both as the founders, separately and together. Please speak freely. Some of the questions are going to be in areas you may want to come back to as you have the opportunity to think about them," Roger said, guiding the couple. "What we'll work toward is your views on your own situation. Most helpful would be to get you to the point where you can create your own guesstimate of what an F^3 model would look like for you."

"There are no right answers or high scores given for being the couple that completes this the fastest. However, at this time what we need is to get your gut feel on where you stand," Carrie added. "Some of the answers to our questions will need to be made with the assistance and scrutiny of your existing professional advisors. It will be necessary later to stress test some of your thinking and answers to these questions.

"With your permission and authorization, we'll be contacting your advisors to obtain your tax returns, investment statements, key legal structural documents and banking information so we can review them to get an accurate picture of your current legal and financial situation. We hope this will save you the headache of having to assemble them yourselves," she said.

"Also, would you mind if we also gather some other detailed information to help us with our assessment? In addition to the legal stuff I just mentioned, we'd like to look at your current net worth statement and your personal spending history."

"Well, that sounds good, because I'm interested in understanding the bigger picture, but not so interested in doing the tabulating," Dan admitted, approving the approach.

"It will be important to stress test your existing legal and financial position against the various succession options that are identified through the F³ succession process."

Throughout the morning, Carrie and Roger asked the Fortunes a series of wide-ranging questions designed to assess the couple's feelings of independence from FCI. The first part was primarily financial perspectives. The conversation continued through the next few hours.

They agreed to break at the midway point of the day and then focus on the Fortunes' emotional independence from the business.

Both parts of this discussion would take into account themselves and their needs as well as their desire to provide for the next generations. FCI would have to be considered as well, as it was the operating company that had built the family nest egg.

"Marnie and Dan, if you thought of your day-to-day lifestyle needs, how much of your required cash flow comes from FCI or related business entities directly or through salary, dividends and company 'perks'?"

For Dan, hearing this was slightly jarring at first, but he could see the wisdom in the discussion being forthright and real. He figured that, with this approach, he and Marnie were in a type of laboratory. It felt like the four of them were talking about someone else.

Marnie led off. "I can't describe to you how effective this is for me, to do what we have done so far, and I'm looking forward to participating with the children in the family piece. Let's face it, though—I'm not so engaged in FCI anymore. It was something this guy hoodwinked me into when we first started seeing each other," she said, nudging Dan and placing her hand atop his.

"He said he had a small food market in this small town and that it had been in the family for a bit. The day we met, he was quitting school to go back and help his mother when Double F passed away. Now *there's* a man who'd be pretty startled if he came back to life. He would have been pretty proud of you, Danny."

"We really don't need the income from what we get from our roles at FCI," Dan interjected, clearly not as comfortable as Marnie in surmising the thinking of his late father. Over the years, Dan had often wondered in private moments about just what Fletcher Fortune would have thought.

His mother had still been alive when the growth years at FCI were ramping up. She had passed away shortly after FCI had launched the *Old Grocers* salad dressing line, with her late husband on the label in his starched white apron. She'd been pleased that Dan had acknowledged this link to his past even though his relationship with Double F had been filled with conflict.

Dan wanted to get back to the question. "So just to be clear here, you're asking about our FCI pay, fees we pay for club memberships and any other distributions such as dividends made solely to either of us?"

Roger's reply took a much more holistic direction than Dan had anticipated. "We'll get to any income you derive from investments in time, but at this point let's keep the focus on the income flowing to you both as a result of the operating company. In determining how much money you'll require, we need to assess together what you have coming in and what those funds get directed to now.

"After your succession, you'll want to continue to maintain a certain lifestyle, and very few people want their lives to change too much. As we look forward from here, this discussion should include how much is required, not only for your personal consumption, but also for eventual estate equalization purposes with the next generation.

"Many people in your position fund charitable causes and you may have some you've historically supported. You may want to think about securing the company for the benefit of the communities in which FCI is a major employer. You'll have to also consider what assets and resources you have available to fund these future needs. At this stage it's timely to assess the extent to which you are dependent on the business to do so. How might these existing sources of personal funds be affected as your future role or ownership position changes?"

At this point, Dan held up his hand as if to get everyone's attention. "Roger, I'd like to comment on what you just said about the communities we operate in. It's very important to me that FCI continues to remain anchored in my home community, to benefit those employees and the community who depend on us.

"The townspeople supported me when, frankly, I felt at the end of my rope. Even though it's been almost fifty years, winning them back and then hearing how those less mobile in town were so appreciative to be able to shop locally makes me emotional. That location is not our biggest or our most profitable, but our decisions must always recognize the impact of that location—the impact of what we did in that town and what that town did for me."

Giving those gathered at the table time to consider Dan's wishes, Carrie brought the room back to the process. "Ultimately, your financial dependence on the business will be one of the key factors in determining what succession option is the right one for you." She reached into a folder to give the Fortunes a sheet of paper with some of the considerations outlined as questions. She also gave them a copy of the notes they were speaking from so they could be clear on where they were going with this part of the discovery process.

"We will eventually get to the point where we ask you to plot yourselves on the *Founder* arm of the F^3 model. We recommend our clients get the clarity for starting this process by preparing a personal net worth statement and listing assets into three broad categories:"

1. Lifestyle Assets

    These include all assets that are held primarily, or only, for lifestyle purposes, so you don't count on a financial return from them.

These are often depreciating assets with the future value declining. Lifestyle assets often also have carrying costs associated with their ongoing use and enjoyment. For example, cars have insurance, and houses and cottages have property taxes and upkeep. Boats, yachts and private planes and their operating costs can also be in the mix.

Examples: houses, cottages, cars, private aircraft, boats, yachts etc.

"These largely drive the cost of maintaining your lifestyle," Roger noted.

Marnie said in an aside to Dan, "Uh, yes, we have some of this stuff, don't we?"

"You're the one we bought the plane for, remember?" he replied, smiling. "Think of the traffic gridlock we've flown over to get to that nice cottage lifestyle," he reminded her.

Roger took note of their comments and weighed in with, "Similarly, it's necessary to assess if, and to what degree, 'corporate living' is taking place. You may lose access to the same kinds of compensation in this department, something that can add quite a bit to your personal lifestyle expenses. We'll assess everything, but let's continue to the potential income from areas outside FCI. Take a look at the second section."

2. Investment Assets *(separate from the business)*

This includes all non–business related investment assets, including tax-sheltered accounts.

Examples: Stock portfolios, real estate holdings (outside of FCI) and any other investments

"Have you put some personal savings and investments aside for yourselves? Rainy day money?" Carrie asked.

The Fortunes had been able to do that after some fairly lean years, where every penny the couple had was poured into the business to meet the shopping center build-outs that FCI was obligated to participate in with Curtis Development Corporation.

Dan had always felt they were late starters as far as putting money into traditional investment vehicles, but nonetheless was happy with what he had done, considering his perception of the volatility.

"With your permission we'll obtain this information from your investment advisors," Carrie said.

> 3. The Business and Related Assets
>
>> This includes the business as well as any real estate and intellectual property used in the business, but it is owned separately. For example, if a separate company, owned by you, owns the property on which the business operates, it must be included in the "Business and Related Assets" section of the net worth statement, as it is still dependent on the business.

"You also want to get a reasonable estimate of the market value of your business in order to have an accurate net worth statement. Think about how much you think it's worth and why. How financially robust is it (market share, profit margins; are they growing, level or shrinking)? How would you assess FCI's customer and supplier relationships? Strategically, are there competitive, technological or industry threats that need to be thought through?"

Roger listed these questions from his head, though they were on the piece of paper in front of Dan. He didn't expect immediate answers, as some needed to be researched, but later on in the day, a gut check analysis would be fine, to help the Fortunes through the model. The primary objective of getting answers to these questions was to figure out whether their net worth met, exceeded or greatly exceeded the estimated cost of funding their future.

"As you can imagine, owners can be quick off the mark with their guesses as to how much their business is worth. Try and look at FCI with the detachment an investor would. What do your present earnings look like? What might they look like in the future? How will some of the current issues you're facing likely affect the value of FCI?

"It's also important to recognize that the role you play in the business is likely to change. For example, you might transition from being the sole owner and executive of the business to acting as the chairman of the board of directors and being one of several shareholders. This transition is often poorly understood and can be badly implemented.

"While a corporate structure is suited to facilitating changes in roles and responsibilities, there are those in similar situations to yours, Dan, who may find it difficult to understand and honour the distinctive role they now hold. This undermines the effectiveness of the transition from a controlling shareholder to a multi-shareholder ownership model."

These points were meaningful to Dan as he thought about the infighting between Fanny and Jeff, which he knew was undermining the confidence of the rest of the management team. Did either realize the damage that this feud could cause to FCI's valuation? *And I haven't even decided how and when I am going to leave yet*, he thought, taking a sip of his coffee.

Roger carried on with his commentary. "This change in roles also affects the compensation you may reasonably expect to receive from the business. For instance, as ownership changes, you'll reduce your involvement in the business and some of your duties may be taken over by new hires; it's therefore critical to know how much it will cost to pay someone to perform the tasks and fill the roles that you or your spouse fill now. This means that looking at your salary or dividends in the past will likely not paint an accurate picture of what future compensation will look like."

The four continued their discussions around these and similar questions throughout the first half of the day. The Fortunes learned that they had to consider the following: inaccuracies in estimating the cost of funding their needs, the impact of inflation on estimating the funding needs, estimating how far their non–business investment assets should go, the fair market value of the business and the predicted returns from the business and portfolio investment assets into the future. Assessing financial dependence or independence would be pivotal in determining what succession options might be open to them.

Marnie looked up from what she was scribbling on her notepad and asked, "Roger, I believe Dan is going to tell you we're fine, and I think so as well, but do you ever find that your clients don't have a good grasp of their financial dependency on the business?"

"Unfortunately, we do see that, Marnie. Sometimes our clients are living good lifestyles, but are more at risk than they realize. It can be disconcerting to discover this fact. It's far better to understand where you are financially at the start of a succession plan than later on, after it's launched, or worse yet, after it has been implemented and you've given up control," he told the couple.

"For instance, if most of your net worth is tied up in the business and the business is barely able to meet your needs, you probably don't have a lot of room for taking on the risks that are often associated with transferring the business within the family. If you wanted the business to stay in the family, one of the family members would likely have to pay full price up front. This severely limits your options.

"On the other hand, at the other end of the spectrum, you may have accumulated sufficient assets outside of the business to meet your goals. If this is the case, you're in a better position to consider succession options that involve keeping the business in the family, depending on what your goals are," Roger stated.

Carrie, sensing that perhaps some encouragement was required, reminded them, "It's important to understand that by avoiding planning your succession you're not serving yourselves or your family's long-term interests. I heard once that the best time to plant an oak tree is fifty years ago, but the second-best time is now. Avoidance is easy to fall into, but will not help with the transition one iota."

Looking past the table, Roger could see Higgins, nose in his paws, getting to his feet with a big stretch. "Before we pause for a break, I'd like to ask you what is emerging here for you."

Marnie went first. "I just feel we're making headway. Between Dan and me, we haven't had too many disconnects with the financial sides of our lives. Let's call a spade a spade. We've been blessed."

To check where Dan was at with the discussion, Roger asked, "Tell me, Dan, was there anything particularly revealing or thought-provoking for you during the founder's financial independence discussion? I'm sure it's a bit of a tug-of-war emotionally for you to consider the question of changing your operational responsibilities."

For Dan, the morning had been enlightening, but he struggled with his own feelings. He had a sense of being a little untethered by it all. "Well, you're right. It's very difficult to get my head around giving up control at this point. I know I don't want to go out the way my father did." He paused to allow his mind to catch up with how he explained his emotions. He looked away slightly, so no one would see his eyes welling up.

"Let's not beat around the bush—I don't need the money. I'll admit my favorite days are when I get out from behind my desk. I get to drive around to the locations and spend time with our staff. I don't care whether it's in the retail locations, the warehouses or the processing plants. I get a big thrill to see it all working. I'm a food guy at heart, not a bigwig executive. I just worked a philosophy, a plan hatched by my friend Ben Curtis. He was the guy with all the vision. I was scared to death. I still am at times. But it all worked out, didn't it."

Dan concluded with a statement followed by a question; both etched in the minds of all there. "What I do need, though, is purpose. I'm not an expert in many things but what I do know is Dan Fortune. I won't be happy unless I mean something to myself and have a purpose. It will kill me if I don't."

He stared around the room, wavering slightly as he looked upon the group. "What and who am I going to be, after all this?" And with that, he grabbed Higgins's leash that was hanging on the coat rack and turned to Carrie. "Can I borrow your pup? I could use a short walk to clear my mind."

"C'mon, Huggles," he said. "Let's get out of here. I see a park right across the street." He strode out of the room.

After Dan was gone for a few moments, the sound of the elevator door opening signaled his departure. In the silence that enveloped the room, Carrie caught her breath and said to no one in particular. "Uh, it's Higgins. His name is Higgins."

Concerned, Marnie made a move to go after her husband. Roger interceded. "Marnie, you know Dan best, but I think he's just blowing off a little steam. He probably needs to reflect alone, and Higgins is the perfect companion. It's amazing what that dog does to people. I find just petting him lowers my stress.

"I saw a piece on the news the other day about these puppy rooms in campus dorms that allow university students to come in and be with the dogs to calm their nerves when studying for final exams. Let's let Dan contemplate things in the break. He'll come back in here refreshed and ready to move on to the next part."

What is Money for?

Dan returned after the break and said aloud, as much to himself as the others, "Money really is about enabling more of life's options, isn't it? I didn't start out to make a lot of money—I just tried to survive. I kept my head down and tried to do the right thing. When it did happen, I found that in most situations, money gave me an extra option and the time and space to make some mistakes while searching for the correct decision."

Marnie looked out the office window, as if to avoid Dan's eye, and said, "I think we did our best and it's been a great ride that isn't over for us. The problem with money …" She looked around the room at the others. "The problem is that sometimes throwing money at a challenge isn't the best course of action. It affected us as parents, I believe. We had this rare resource that many others don't have, to direct at those problems.

"Growing up, my father used to say to us girls that most problems we would face in life were going to be rooted in either time or money. I never really knew what he was trying to tell us at the time, but I've come to realize he was right. I think I was too young, too naive to accept the real message.

"He said that, in his medical practice, sometimes he saw people throw money at health problems that actually required time, which might have been the much harder course of action. Instead, they might have required exercise, physiotherapy, researching food choices or things like that, which required time commitment. He saw patients and families from all walks of life.

"His time and money theory also included family and child-raising problems. It was his experience that some of the more affluent—not all, mind you—occasionally made those time and money mistakes in rearing their children. 'The harder route that takes more time is often best, girls,' he'd tell us."

Thinking back to the wisdom of her late father with a faint smile, Marnie continued. "Many of his patients came in to talk about an ailment but the conversation would drift into family problems. He said that so often the person would leave and the original physical pains were already healing by the end of the visit."

Dan knew she was reflecting on the second generation, specifically Jimmy's recent challenges. Hearing his wife say it further embedded in his mind that they had made mistakes. He hoped that this process would be able to give them a way to treat everyone in the family in an equitable way and that all of the second generation would be able to think of the bigger picture and not just themselves.

The Fortunes also heard other insights that afternoon that gave them fresh perspectives on their situation. First was how their nonfinancial goals and objectives were influencing their financial situation. The second was how interdependent FCI and the family were, and how this had to be taken into consideration.

Carrie broached the grimmer subject of the death of either Dan or Marnie. "One of the pieces that can be evaluated with this scrutiny of your finances is your personal readiness if one or the other of you dies. Think of your total estate holdings: the personal use assets, portfolio assets and business holdings. How is everything owned, and how would you like to see your estate dealt with in the event of your passing away?

"What financial provisions are necessary in a first-to-die scenario for either of you? Some people we've worked with assign personal use and portfolio assets to the other surviving spouse and business assets to the next generation and/or for charitable purposes," Carrie explained. "That's just one of the many options.

"We also need to consider taxes. We'll look at the planning you've done in this area. Have you thought about how to defer the taxes on this or how these taxes are to be funded?"

Dan replied with a slow nod. "We did some planning but I'm not really sure how it works."

"As part of this process, we'll investigate the approach you've taken to this point, get details, assess and report back," Roger said. "Dan, you said earlier that you'd like to see the business remain headquartered here in the city and kept in the family for your grandchildren. How do you see this working? What could go wrong?"

At this, Dan shrugged. During his walk with Higgins, he'd started to see the value of getting a tighter grip on his succession.

"Have we really discussed these plans with the children?" Marnie asked Dan, now moving in her chair to look at her husband fully. "I would like to make sure they don't feel they're being drafted as 'involuntary partners' into FCI."

"Some families have goals in place around charitable causes and put various vehicles in place to give effect to the charitable portion of their wishes," Roger said. "There are many creative and effective ways to give back both within and outside of the business. Such activities can nurture individuals and help instill the values you feel are important in future generations, as well as allow for a shared family vision and more cohesion."

At this point, Marnie turned to Dan. "You know something? It will be nice to get Inge in here and get her perspective. She really does have some good ideas, and the foundation is starting to generate some positive results. We did put a foundation in place that, as an initial project, funded part of the new wing of the art gallery here in the city," Marnie said. "Inge, our younger daughter, has been looking after our family's charitable giving for the last few years."

"You know, I've been thinking of reviewing that foundation," Dan added. "It's not that I think Inge is doing something wrong; her heart is in the right place. But I don't know that what she chooses to get us involved in properly reflects our entire family and what we collectively value."

The couple was asked to reflect on other questions that were more focused on the personal imprint they would leave on others. How would each like to be remembered? By family, the community, FCI employees, Dan's industry colleagues, their friends …?

In order to help the Fortunes transition from a business perspective to a personal perspective on their future, they were also asked to think about how they spent time outside of FCI. Between Roger and Carrie, they asked the Fortunes questions like, "What do you like to do together? Who are your friends and where are they located now? What do you have in common and like to do together?"

Dan explained that his peer group were those he had met doing business over the years. Some went way back, like Ben Curtis, and some were entrepreneurs that were part of the CDC projects.

Others were those he had met at some of the grocers' industry convention. They were a mixture of suppliers and distributors as well as others with similar operations to FCI. Those guys he remembered as a pretty entertaining group who were a lot of fun, and he still enjoyed getting together with them. They were spread apart geographically and didn't see each other as much these days, he added.

He disclosed that he and Marnie had belonged to a golf club for a long time. She loved the place, he noted, but his own opportunities to actually golf depended on the season, and he hoped to do more of that in the coming years. He concluded with a story about having to leave team sports, which he'd loved, due to the demands of his work schedule.

"I loved playing all the team sports I could get involved with as a boy. You learn so much through working with others to reach common objectives or goals in any team game," Dan reminded the group.

"I had to cut myself off from any sport where I was part of other people's schedules, when I took the old Market over. It wasn't fair to the others, who were expecting a full team to show up, and to play short every week. That's why golf interested me because I could control the schedule better," he reminisced.

"Now our son Jim was never interested in sports, but Jeff played everything and is still involved in the men's rec leagues we have in the area. I've always reminded Jeff that he has a job as well, and not to forsake that. I was happy he enjoyed sports, but had to occasionally remind him not to get involved if he was taking someone else's spot and then wasn't able to show up regularly to play."

Marnie wanted to say something, but waited to allow Dan to finish his thoughts. She knew that because her husband had so successfully divorced himself from activities he'd previously enjoyed, he felt that everyone else shared his values and priorities. However, she also knew that her son felt that his father was in the dark ages. Healthy competition outside the office was good for the mind, body and soul, Jeff said, and she agreed. I'm working to live and not living to work, he would tell her when he and his father conflicted on his schedule.

"Beyond my friends that golf," Marnie said, "there are so many I'm connected to that are wonderful people." She raised her eyes to the ceiling, visualizing her own circle. "Now you have me thinking that things can change and I can't wait till I get a bit more of my husband's time," she said, glancing at Dan. "One of the great things about golf is that with the handicap system both men and women can play an enjoyable round together—even compete, if that's so important," she said with a smile, reaching out to nudge Dan's elbow.

"Is the fact that Marnie would like to spend more time together a surprise to you, Dan?" Roger asked.

"No ... no, it's not. I have heard that," was his quiet response.

"Beyond that group, who else do you like to spend time with, Marnie?" Carrie asked.

"Well," Marnie said, "I've often met friends through causes here in the community and through the people who had children around the age of our kids. Believe me, I won't be changing my social scene in this succession. Listen, this guy couldn't get enough of my time when we met. My hope is that Dan can spend more time with me and that between all the great people we both know together and individually, we can keep active."

"Here are some areas you need to give thought to. Think of any additional costs to take into consideration, including legal and support obligations as well as risk minimization. While nobody wants to anticipate legal obligations, such as a breakdown in the marriage, it is important to understand that not preparing for the possibility can have severe ramifications for the business, particularly if the business was built during the time of the marriage."

At this point, Dan waved his finger at his wife and said with a smile, "Don't even think of leaving me now."

Marnie gave her husband a shy smirk and said, "Well, you're going to need me to continue to get you out of the messes you create."

Now approaching the whiteboard where the hand-drawn scale was labeled "Founders Independence," Roger asked, "Can you both give us an individual gut reaction to two perspectives? Therefore on the scale as drawn, please plot along the *Founders* leg how independent you feel from FCI, from both a financial and nonfinancial perspective. You can see that it's numbered from 0 to 10. Zero is totally dependent and 10 is totally independent, but clients commonly feel they are somewhere in between."

The Fortunes conferred for several minutes before Marnie went up and plotted two numbers. "At this point, we both feel we're 9 out of 10 on our feeling of financial independence. That may change when we get your independent assessment back on those areas that you spoke of. At this point, though, count us as blissfully unaware of any trouble in that area," she said, smiling and crossing her fingers. "Dan, you plot us on our emotional independence. The way I see it, that area is much more you than me."

Dan stood up, marker in hand. "As I said earlier, I'm struggling with giving this up and I can tell you that I'm not sure at all. I want to say I'm on the fence and give us a 5, but I can't really say it's even that high. What staying involved as I do means to me is worth far more than getting a salary. I've been fortunate to see some topnotch organizations in our business. I know there are some very sharp people out there and that I'm replaceable.

"However, acknowledging that and then being able to step away operationally is a tough one. I am giving us—I guess, me—a 2."

Fortune - Founder's F³® Self Assessment

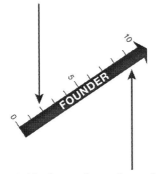

Emotional Independence from the firm

Financial Independence from the firm

Gaining Other Perspectives

"Now Tom Coyle will tell you there are other issues on the business side that should also be taken into consideration during succession planning," Roger said as he resumed his overview. "Often, when you, the owner, leave the business, there's a period of instability during which there's a lack of effective leadership. This can cause a necessary drain on the financial resources of the business to replace the 'know-how' that has been lost, among other expenses."

Now it was Dan's turn to tease Marnie. "I am basically irreplaceable, don't you think?"

"Later in the week, we're going to get the people in your family and from FCI that you designate to come in that should be there working with us to focus on your operating company," Roger said. "Who are those key people?"

Dan thought for a moment about who should join them. He started to speak and then paused again, moving his head from side to side as if to balance his thoughts before responding. "Well, I guess myself; that's kind of obvious isn't it. RJ should be here in her capacity as head of operations. She's trying to retire again herself, so we're going to have a huge hole to fill there.

"Let's get Fanny and Jeff involved as I'm sure they'll have thoughts on what to do. I guess that means you should join us as well then, Marnie, in case all hell breaks loose," he added with a short, nervous chuckle.

Marnie responded sharply, "Oh, thanks. I probably have some other value, though, as I was around from the start. Don't forget that. And you should also have Peter, or is he away on one of his trips?" she said, thinking of her brother-in-law and his ability to enjoy his life since retiring.

Dan was now considering others. "Let's get Bill Finch, our CFO. He has a great way of interpreting numbers and is a solid thinker. I'd also like to bring a store guy for that perspective. They are on the ground every day. The kid I'm thinking of is going to be 'C-suite' one day. I'll ask him, if you feel it makes sense."

Counting on his fingers quickly, he said, "That makes seven so far. Tell you what: I'll ask RJ which one of her operations people we should have with us. She's always telling me she has the odd one that stands out."

"I'll tell you who we need: it's Ben Curtis. I know he can't come, but that man makes it all so simple," Marnie added.

At this point, Roger was encouraged to see that the Fortunes were engaged and thinking about what getting the correct perspectives and information meant to them. However, it was now necessary to rein them in slightly and not try to cover too much ground on this day. These were areas of life that were simply difficult to think about.

"I can tell you, I was talking with one of Ben's people on something for the Curtis family just yesterday. It would be impossible for Ben to come. He's going to expand his UWI medical scholarship program and is right now at the main campus working with their people to set that up."

"Yeah," Dan admitted, "that would have been a bit like completing a 'hail Mary pass' to bring him in at this point, wouldn't it? I can just see him shooing me away like he always did in the early days, reminding me that I already knew what to do. 'Just stay out of your own way,' he would say."

"I agree with Ben. It sounds like you have the people we need already, and it's your show," Roger assured him. He continued. "Well from our end, I can tell you that Tom Coyle will be back with us to lead the *Firm* day. Tom's focus is on ensuring that the operating company's needs are properly reflected in the overall succession plan. I will be here, but Carrie will sit that session out to work on compiling some of your personal financial pieces that we covered this morning. She'll be needed to take calls from some of the professionals you work with, as we start our activity with them this week as well."

In anticipation of the day focused solely on FCI, Dan would be advised to consider the following questions: What were FCI's management team's strengths? What strengths did he see in himself? Where were the gaps and areas for improvement? What was his overall philosophy about being in business? Which management styles and concepts did he believe in and which did he feel less enthused about? Did he feel senior FCI people added value to each other or not? These questions were just a start on where he would be taken before the assessment of the FCI component was complete.

"Marnie, Dan, we'll also get your thoughts at this point on two simple questions about FCI. Taking into account FCI's customer and supplier relationships, how independent do you feel the company is, without you working day to day? The second is how you feel at this point about the company's financial strength and resiliency. Where is it financially?" Roger asked.

"You can use your answers to plot a point on the *Firm* arm of the F^3 model. You may be influenced to how you see the *Firm* arm now, considering what we spoke about today with your financial and emotional independence. Remember, your own numbers on this arm of F^3 may change once you get the feedback of your FCI leadership team on that day, but what we need is how you feel today."

This time, Marnie stayed rooted in her chair and let Dan address both perspectives up on the whiteboard.

"I'm wondering now how the score I give FCI might change when we hear from the others, but let's go with these numbers for right now."

Fortune - FCI F³® Self Assessment

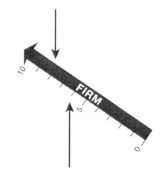

Dan's intensity was evident as he looked at the others. "On our relationship side, I'm giving FCI a 6. This is because I now realize that perhaps I haven't exposed others to enough of our supply side relationships that are outside of FCI itself. We have built up our distribution over the years, and we have FCI-owned subsidiaries sourcing a lot of what goes on the shelves. Our senior people—well, mainly RJ—go to some of the high-level industry events, but I get a lot of calls that I think could be handled by others.

"With our customer relationships, I am also troubled a bit. Until recently, all our ads were either me talking about our locations or my voiceover on all our product spots or radio ads. I haven't really thought of how valuable it would have been to involve more of the staff in the media spots. Why was I there talking about why our produce is so fresh when Jeff understands it so much better?"

Dan continued, "I would love to tell you that our financial strength and resiliency is a 10, but in this one area, I wouldn't give 10s, even on good days. There's always something that could be better. It's been my experience that when I felt that things were all figured out, it was the exact moment that something happened to prove me wrong.

"I'm happy enough with the financial controls in place, and the reporting I receive on where we're at. However, I can't say that everyone really understands the financial picture like they should. I've been looking for a way to build financial acumen in every department of FCI. It would mean a lot to us if we could give everyone a fundamental business education," he concluded.

Roger now moved Dan back to the matter at hand. "So what grade would you give the financial strength and resiliency of FCI?"

"I'm going with 7. We must be diligent in that area," the founder said before seating himself back at the round meeting table.

Carrie had been attending to something in the outer office, but had now joined them in the meeting room. "It's getting late, but before we stop, we're going to come back to your family and ask you to reflect on that as well. This step is not considered definitive for now, but your mutual consensus on how you see your family's affinity for each other is valuable to the succession planning process."

The Next Generation: Who, How and Why

Drawing everyone's attention to the *Family* arm of the F^3 model, Roger asked, "Dan, Marnie, we also want your thoughts on how connected you feel members of the second generation may or may not be to FCI."

"In essence, you're being asked to assess your feelings about where the next generation is coming at this from. They'll be coming in as a group through this process. It's appropriate to isolate your own perspective from theirs, in advance of that," Carrie said.

In the concluding conversation of the day, some of the questions they considered were: What would you describe as your family's shared values? What are the strengths, weaknesses and interests of each person in the family? Can you describe their personal styles, attributes and motivators? How does your family get along with each other and with each of you? What is the nature of your relationship with each? How interested and involved are each of your children in FCI? How dependent are they on FCI (financially, emotionally, socially)?

Both Carrie and Roger had noticed that when the Fortunes were asked questions, Dan would usually draw back to give his wife a chance to express her opinion first. He would listen to what she said and then fill in his own thoughts. It was common for Marnie to then offer the nuance that confirmed their mutual opinion.

Thus Marnie led into the discussion of their family. "I can tell you that Fanny is Dan's child and is Fortune through and through. I never knew Dan's father but I'm told that there are many similarities between Fanny and her grandfather. From what I've heard about Double F, they share a tendency to sometimes miss the small social graces of interpersonal skills. She has led our family in many ways, and as a young girl, pressed for Dan's attention until she got it. He was always busy with FCI. It would have been easy for a child to feel adrift from her dad, but not Fanny."

"She would pepper me with questions and requests whenever she had the chance. I couldn't be in the door ten seconds before it started," Dan said, smiling. "And I can tell you," he added, his brow creasing slightly, "Fanny didn't take no for an answer. I can remember very few instances where she didn't get her way.

"I'm concerned that the situation at work is just an evolution of this behavior of pressing too hard and that sense of urgency that reaches into every aspect of her life. I have that as well, I guess, but it needs to be filtered if you're going to be effective with other people," Dan explained.

"I can also tell you I love her spirit and that she's valuable to us at FCI. She is among the very best, if not the best we have at getting something finished, as long as she isn't relying on others. She'll butt heads with anyone and everyone, but she will deliver a result within a short time span. I guess I'd say that with Fanny you'll get your omelet, but always with broken eggs.

"I'm continually impressed with what she has done for us politically. There are a lot of regulatory issues in the food industry and so there should be. There's nothing more important about being a human being than what we take into our bodies. There aren't a lot of people who can get the type of reaction from government she can. This thing with Jeff was her seeing an opening to cast her influence over another piece of the business with these upcoming health department regulations." Dan now looked to Marnie for some help in describing their headstrong daughter.

Marnie added, "Fanny measures herself against others by financial success and by possessions. She wants to win. Her agenda is her agenda and she would prefer that others respect it and not mess with it. If she's not in charge then you're probably not going to maintain her interest for long," Marnie explained. "I think this fight with Jeff is that need to control things, but it appears to be beyond her to mask it in any way."

"We both feel that in Al, she married a really good guy who appears to have unlimited reserves of resiliency. He's a stoic who understands what he needs to add with their children and just quietly goes about his business," Dan added. "I'll also say that at this point, they are certainly living well. Al has an avid interest in investing, but in the market of the last couple of years I'm not sure how he has fared. He came into their relationship with a small investment portfolio that he scrimped and saved to accumulate. At least he's aware of the importance of money management. He doesn't get recognition for that side too much, but I can tell you I noticed it. He has never come to me for a dime."

"Fanny has faults, like any of us, but I doubt that she's so far off track she can't see the need to rally around her father and this decision to start a succession plan," Marnie concluded.

"Now, who's next? Is it your other daughter or your son Jeff?" Carrie asked.

"That would be Jeff, and he's also heavily involved in the business," Marnie confirmed.

"He could be called the 'smartest Fortune ever'," his mother said, clearly proud that Jeff had inherited what she saw as the Farver intellect. "Jeff is the family conscious, I think. His wife Jennifer is a Curtis as you may be aware. She has always encouraged him to positively assert himself, and when he senses trouble, he's the first to try and help. We saw this again when Jimmy ran into his trouble, didn't we, Dan?"

Dan nodded. "Jeff's a capable executive as well. He's the exact opposite of his older sister, really. The Jeff I see at work is collaborative to a fault. He likes to win together and sometimes that comes back to bite him. He can be drawn off the mission of the day by being overly analytical, I think, at times. I've always expected that he would grow out of that with regard to FCI but I haven't seen it yet. I was once a little more like that, early on, but there's a time when decisions have to be made.

"I won't be telling him what to do. I know that if he confronts Fanny on areas where he sees her moving too far into his responsibilities she'll back off. Fanny respects those who assert themselves and will mow down those who don't," Dan said, as he identified the crux of the FCI feud.

Now smiling broadly, Dan said, "Financially, Jeff is capable, and in the longer term being married to a Curtis is not going to hurt him. He and Jennifer don't have many money worries, though he tells me he likes getting his money from FCI. I guess having five children is more expensive than just four like us," he added, with a pointed nod at Marnie.

"Maybe it's the recognition factor from just getting a regular income for his contributions to the firm, Dan," Marnie said.

Dan shook this suggestion off, mentally trying to establish his point of view on his eldest son and to be fair to him. "Listen, at the end of the day, he's a steady guy, and steadiness is valuable in an industry like ours. Maybe it's just me, but not everything needs to be such a big deal. My motto is 'make the decision and move on.' Live with the result. Jeff can be a victim of 'paralysis of analysis,' if you've heard that term before."

Marnie countered her husband's view. "Jeff just wants to please you, Dan. He wants to earn your respect." With a raised eyebrow toward Dan as she spoke sharply, she said, "For God's sake, he's an engineer. When you're the lead dog, you can make these compromises. If he made these calls, wouldn't you be all over him?"

To Roger and Carrie, the Fortune matriarch described her son in a more intuitive way. "Jeff is analytical first and foremost and could have reached any academic goal he wanted. Learning comes very easily to him, I think. It's sometimes hard for him to let something go that he knows can be improved upon. I know that what he comes up with on these food-borne disease threats—which is what started this feud—will be industry leading. FCI has had a history with innovation in the food industry that is highly regarded; it's been recognized with awards. The last thing Jeff wants is to take shortcuts on what needs to be done and cause FCI or our family to lose face. He'll solve this in his own thorough way."

Clearly upset now with what she perceived as Dan's lack of empathy with Jeff, she rounded back on her husband. "That kid needs a little support here. Forget this 'he has to stand up to his sister' stuff. You know that Jeff will extend himself to others to the detriment of himself at times, but I don't want to see him hardened to the point where he isn't the son I love."

Seeing that Marnie was a little flushed and that Dan looked like he had just received the verbal equivalent of a cuff to his head, Roger changed course.

"Let's talk about"—and he looked down to his notes—"your daughter, Inge. Tell us about her style and what she lives her life to do."

Glad to be saved from the previous discussion, Dan led off this time on his younger daughter. "Well, you would have thought when she was a girl that she could have anything she wanted in life."

Counting now on his fingers, Dan spoke about his younger daughter with pride. "Inge is intuitively smart, beautiful, confident, well-spoken and concerned with helping others in the world. She had every option possible, but she chose a different course than I would have. She wasn't helped by her marriage to the Finnish guy, though. That guy cost us as much emotionally as financially and I can tell you, the financial was too big."

"Norwegian," Marnie corrected him. And then turning to Carrie and Roger, "I just want to keep our facts straight, I mean for the record, anyway."

Marnie took over. "Inge is a free spirit who loves the art world. She values form, harmony, beauty and self-expression over just about anything else. She'll sit back and take her time in working through something slowly but consistently. She shares Jeff's humanitarian approach with others, although not to his extent. She wants to do things for others and that's why we made the philanthropic gesture to assist in funding the new wing of the gallery.

"She made the gallery a personal mission after her marriage fell apart, as she was really down at the time and felt she had made no impact in her life. We knew she would follow it through. She will complete a task and then move on to another as long as she's truly interested in the task's objective."

"I think the challenge we have with Inge is that she doesn't really seem that interested in how money gets made or where it comes from in our family," Dan said with a career business person's factuality.

"When she was in high school, we put her on the bakery counter at one of the locations. We came to realize through her supervisor that her cake decorating was a little too good and the supervisor wasn't getting half the productivity out of Inge that she did with the other part time staff. This was brought to her attention and she walked out on the spot, muttering about restrictions on her artistic freedom," a bemused Dan told them, shaking his head.

"She's currently very committed to our family community programs. All this philanthropy is nice, but we need to put a business case around that foundation or, over time, we'll all become disengaged in its purpose."

"How about Jimmy?" Carrie now interjected. "How does he fit into all this?"

Marnie let out a breath and exchanged a quick glance with Dan. "Jimmy's got a heart of gold but he's perhaps chosen the wrong crowd at times. Certainly in his adult life, anyway, which resulted in some of the trouble he was involved in recently."

"At his request, he has moved back with us and is staying in the guest house right on the property."

Considering what he'd read in the newspaper pertaining to Jimmy Fortune, Roger wondered how his brother and sisters felt about the youngest Fortune. He was about to broach just that subject with Dan when Marnie continued.

"I believe Jimmy's siblings consider him a 'failure to launch' at this point, and he needs to redeem himself in their eyes. They would also describe him as a bit of an unknown, due to the differences in ages. Fanny is a full 15 years older than him, so they've never had much of a connection at all. All three are concerned for him, but also feel that he needs to get a direction sooner rather than later," Marnie explained.

Dan took over the background overview. "He's very aware of money and what it will do. In the last few years, Jim has partially funded himself by buying and selling hard-to-find parts for classic cars, boats and planes. He's always had an interest in car restoration. He was telling me that he'd like to be able to get into some kind of business around that. I told him, why not consider boats and small planes as well, as he's been around them enough. I can tell you I've spent a lot on maintenance of exactly those types of possessions over the years and might want to co-invest if the right situation came along."

Dan let Marnie have the last word. "The one other thing about Jimmy that's so unique is his spirituality. He seems to have more of a connection to a higher power than the rest of us. By the way, you may be thinking that his recent brush with the law has something to do with that, but it doesn't. This is not new. He attended a high school where religion was part of the curriculum and just became interested in what it all meant for him."

"How do they all get along?" Carrie asked, now feeling that the parents had given a good background on each of the next generation.

Dan started to reply, a notch too loud. "Well, if we could get the two at FCI to stop—" He stopped when he saw his clearly agitated wife raise her hand to gain his attention.

"Dan Fortune, how about we face the facts here? I don't think all our issues involve just Fanny and Jeff. They aren't all about Jimmy, your emotional dependency on FCI or the financial, tax and legal ramifications of whatever we choose to do in this succession plan.

"Ben said it best, didn't he: succession has to be a people process, above all. Just talking through this has enlightened me on the finer points of what a family business has to think through. We're not the only ones the GBA people see that have a few problems in getting something like this done. I suspect there are many with next generations, a founder with a similar profile to yours and a company with a workforce and customer base that is dependent on this going right."

Marnie paused looking across the table for confirmation from Roger and Carrie, who nodded. "Dan, in order to make this work, we're going to need the other's input, but for now, at the very least, I think we have a good idea on our own perspectives going forward. Do you?"

After Marnie's outburst, Dan looked up at the ceiling for a moment and then, giving those in the room his attention, said a quiet, "Yes."

Roger smiled, sensing that nerves were a little frayed, but not unexpectedly. It had been a long day and they'd asked the Fortunes to cover a lot of territory.

"Now we need you to consider where you are on the *Family* arm of the F^3 model. You should take two things into consideration. Think of each of the children, individually and then collectively. The first consideration then is to plot their collective affinity for the family and each other. Then separately think of their independence—financially and emotionally—from the company."

Marnie rose to her feet and said, "I'd like to take a stab at the affinity for family." She paused as she picked up the marker and gathered her thoughts, looking like she wanted to think it through as she plotted the score. She turned back to the others and quietly said, "This is hard to do, and I guess when we get the family in the room it could change, but I've been through the wringer on just about every front lately. I've felt I've let my family down in letting it get out of hand."

Carrie, having the advantage of her own feminine insight, felt Marnie could do with some female empathy. "Marnie, it may not surprise you to hear that many clients air some family dirty laundry. Some situations are pretty severe. If those troubles or dirty laundry were all hanging on a clothesline together along with your own, and you could take another person's, you would probably take your own troubles back. Just getting to know you both tells me you both have what it takes to work things through," she said.

Marnie dabbed her eyes and smiled to acknowledge Carrie for her comment. "Well, I still can't give us more than a 5, but I'm hopeful it can be made better through all this."

Now Dan joined her. "I've been thinking through the question of the next generation's affinity for FCI. By the way, I agree with you, Marnie; there's work to be done with everyone. The way I see it, we have two of the family interested in FCI and two that wouldn't want that life for themselves. I need to be equitable and maybe I can support them in different ways.

"With regard to Fanny and Jeff, if you feel somehow to blame, it's more me that should be blamed. FCI is my domain and I should have recognized this problem in its earlier stages. Actually, I did see it in its earlier stages and didn't take action. If it had been two senior executives not named Fortune, I think things might have been different. I failed you and them.

"And as for Inge and Jimmy, I know they don't want to be involved, but I share your feelings on our responsibility to foster an accountability in them to have purposeful lives," he concluded.

"In my mind I'm going to give the Fortunes a 5. Let's leave it open though until our family gets involved in this. I feel that the older two make their contribution to FCI and deserve their financial independence in some form.

We'll have to see what form that takes. Inge and Jim are the two I want to hear from when we meet as a family. I have something in mind for both, but let's wait and hear from them first.

"When would you and Tom want to meet with the FCI people, Roger?" Dan asked.

The Lunch

"Tom Coyle, what took you so long?" Dan Fortune said, laughing, as he reached across the restaurant booth to shake hands. "I was up early this morning thinking about this. I wanted us to have some privacy to talk, so I arrived early to grab my regular table. I think when the lunch crowd dissipates we'll be able to have a good chat."

In taking Dan's outstretched hand, Tom took note that while Dan attempted to project an air of nonchalance, he was nervous, perhaps uncharacteristically so. The pair had agreed to meet for lunch before the session in the coming days with the FCI executive team at the GBA offices.

For the *Firm*-focused meeting, Tom had requested that he and Dan get together to go over a format that Tom liked to use in these meetings. The objective was to cover the various visions of what FCI could be from the perspective of each in attendance. Tom had found this kind of feedback helpful, and thought Dan could get clarity on how others saw things, juxtaposed against his own viewpoint.

Tom knew that Dan and Marnie had given the *Firm* arm of the F^3 model a noncommittal score when they'd met at GBA with Roger and Carrie. He thought the low score in the area of the firm's independence was a manifestation of Dan's unease with leaving, coupled with his personal pain from the conflict between Fanny and Jeff.

Tom was hungry and ordered quickly. He was happy to have the chance to talk with Dan about his business. He knew most of the history of FCI, but wanted to hear Dan verbalize it again; he'd never met an entrepreneur of Dan's stature who didn't love to tell the war story about making it to the top. A careful listen would often reveal what would be important in the business-level piece of the succession plan.

"You know, I would have been happy to host at my office, Tom, and bring in something catered from the commissary. No trouble for me—we're in the food business," reminded Dan, smiling at his own irony.

"Yes, I did get that message from Miss Tibbs. We'll have to do that at some point. However, I thought it was important to get both of us out of the office. A neutral environment can free the mind; not being interrupted by anything like phones, texts and emails can be helpful," Tom said. "What we need to cover today requires you to wear your CEO/president hat only. We'll eventually need to give equal and independent status to the firm in the GBA plan."

Just then, the servers arrived with their lunch and the two tucked in, saving the business conversation until afterwards. Both enjoyed the lunch, while exchanging some memories and critiques on golf courses that each had played.

They had ordered coffee when Tom settled back into the confines of the booth. "So tell me about the food industry and how FCI carved out its niche. I heard the tough circumstances of how you came to be in the business when your father passed away. Tell me, though, what have you learned from getting from then to now?"

The restaurant gradually cleared, and the day staff noted that other than ordering a refill or two, the two gentlemen stayed rooted in their conversation. Words got around in the kitchen that the older man was Mr. Fortune, the founder of Fortune Consolidated, the company that supplied the restaurant with some of its fare.

In Tom's experience with companies like FCI, one of the keys to obtaining the right input was the design of the meeting format. That design's objective was to avoid executive mitigation. Tom had seen several situations where founders in Dan's situation could cause mitigation of the facts with their strength of personality alone.

"Dan, I'm sure you've heard the term 'mitigation' before, particularly when someone is trying to communicate something potentially risky," Tom said.

"Yes, I have. It's when people start to make excuses," Dan replied at once.

Tom had at times directed his clients to a dictionary to look up the word. One would find something like *"Mitigation is the action of reducing the severity, seriousness or painfulness of something."*

Tom knew that mitigation was the cause of many disconnects within a family enterprise. It could be found in the family itself and may, at the same time, be evident in those non-related professional managers. These disconnects take the form of a deference to authority that doesn't serve the greater purpose of the enterprise and often holds progress back, all to avoid being perceived as the bearer of bad news.

At an operational level, errors in communication and the ability to execute agreed-upon strategy and direction will often occur if pursuing this process of openness is ignored.

"Most people are risk averse. It may appear as though someone's making excuses, but the question then is why do they feel the need to try, isn't it?" Tom explained.

"Yes, I have seen it over the years. People sometimes do feel the need to sugarcoat the truth," Dan acknowledged, nodding. "Why the hell do people feel the need to do that?"

"We mitigate when we're being polite, or when we're ashamed or embarrassed, or when we're being deferential to authority. It can be caused by the target if he or she reacts explosively to bad news," Tom answered. "Do you think that might be happening with you?"

Dan looked back across the table before responding. "Yes, I would be jobbing you if I said I react positively to everything I hear. It wouldn't be normal, would it?"

"It can be a challenge for anyone," Tom said. "Later on, if you'd like, we can do some work in self-awareness and self-understanding, with you and any others who are interested. It's truly a major leap when you combine all you've accumulated in business knowledge, management acumen and formal education with personal insight on your highest performing style. Gaining better clarity on self and in your communication with others is a winning mix."

Tom continued, moving the conversation back to the *Firm* arm of the F^3 model. "If we can truly unravel how each person sees FCI, it can give us, especially you, remarkable clarity on the operational side of the business and the group's commitment to being part of a change like this. Within the succession planning process, the Fortune family, including both Marnie and you, can be much more efficient if you can establish an environment of trust," Tom said.

"I'm going to ask your group for their individual perspectives. What we need is an overview from each participant on four categories: How they would describe their own and FCI's past, its present and its future, and finally eliciting from each any roadblocks they foresee that could possibly derail the company on the way there.

"This is a solitary exercise done in advance of the session later this week, so that each can speak his or her mind. I've customized a template for FCI and would like to ask you to arrange one-to-one meetings with each of the participants in the next day or two through Miss Tibbs," Tom explained.

"Many people don't tolerate ambiguity very well. These types of meetings can cause angst among executives. They so rarely have a forum in which to state their unfiltered thoughts on how they see things.

"My purpose with an initial meeting is to put everyone at ease and explain the process so they can keep focused on making their best contribution without, as you said, sugarcoating anything. Mitigation within a group at a high level in a company like FCI means time wasted if the group feels that commenting on challenges may be unwelcome."

Tom handed Dan the template that he would be giving to all attendees. It was very simple, and each of the four categories that Tom had described was represented, with several sub-questions on each, to encourage clarity.

"So I get to see what everyone else thinks, then," Dan said. "I like that. Am I part of this, too? Can I let them know how I'm seeing it?"

"Yes, of course, and Marnie as well. I'm also asking you both to complete your individual perspectives on the same template as everyone else."

"What happens then?" Dan asked. "Will you be telling us what we need to do to work together on this?"

When Dan heard Tom's response, he gave a surprised start and his eyes opened wide. "No, I won't be. I'll facilitate the process, but these are the people to listen to," was Tom's reply. "This is an opportunity to hear from those within your group who will be making the transfer of operational control happen, if that's one of your options. From what I've heard, you have more options than many founders do.

"The most effective method is for each of you to give a verbal presentation off flip-chart paper, based on the same criteria you have in front of you. Keeping it simple and unintimidating levels the playing field for everyone and makes long strides toward eliminating mitigation. We'll draw straws for order, but you'll go last."

Dan rubbed his brow with a concerned look, taking in what Tom was saying. "Obviously I've had to give occasional presentations over the years within employee and industry associations, but this will be hard for Marnie."

"It won't be a breeze for anybody, Dan, but as long as everyone you've asked to take part is committed to contributing to a solution, they'll be fine. It's not a public speaking contest. Each will be coached to just articulate his or her vision."

Dan still didn't appear convinced.

"If you asked Marnie about how she saw a potential renovation of your cottage very early in the planning stages and you gave her some simple criteria within which she could explain herself, would she be able to tell you how she saw things?" Tom asked.

"Oh, yeah," Dan said, nodding and smiling with his eyes closed.

"Does she know anything about the technical how-to's of what goes into such a project?" Tom continued. "How about operating a backhoe?"

He saw Dan shaking his head.

"No, and she doesn't need to, does she? She needs to explain things from her vantage point. It's no different from your CFO providing his answers within a financial context. That's a home game for him—his natural talent and what he's probably most comfortable with," Tom assured Dan.

"My job, Dan, when I meet with everyone individually, is to assure them that we don't expect them to have the master plan all by themselves. We want to avoid letting anyone feel that kind of pressure. Some may think they do have that plan and may positively influence the room. Unless there's collective purpose and understanding on the overall structure of succession within the firm in the end, we've missed the mark.

"The next time we see each other will be on the day of the firm review, Dan. I look forward to it."

Dan rose from the booth and then paused, checking behind him to find his keys on the cushioned bench. It had been an extended lunch and he'd enjoyed spending time with Tom. However, he thought he would add something to their conversation. "Tom, I want to tell you that you, Roger and Carrie have helped me get to where I am on this so far. I'm getting better clarity through this—better understanding of my options, I think. I can say that being the founder, CEO, president and whatever else you call me is a lonely job sometimes."

"Why is that?" Tom asked. He had heard this sense of being alone countless times from other executives he'd worked with, but wanted to hear Dan articulate it himself. His experience had shown him that this admission was the entry point for an executive like Dan to express his deeper emotions.

"Well, it can be overwhelming at times," Dan continued. "There are network groups for executives and business owners that I've heard can be really helpful, but that trend was introduced a little too late in my career. My group was sometimes just me and a few shots from a bottle of Jack at the end of the day."

"Have you spoken with Marnie about this?"

Sitting back down and beckoning Tom to do the same, Dan unloaded his thoughts. "Well, as much as possible, I keep to myself on it. It can look like I'm lashing out at times if it gets to be too much for me."

"I guess my family's expectation has always been that I am this rock that just endures whatever gets sent my way. I do that for the most part, I guess. It's not always easy, though," Dan said, wondering if he'd made himself a little too vulnerable in Tom's eyes.

Tom sensed that Dan might be feeling like his disclosure was unique and wanted to make sure he left Dan at ease and with a clear head on it. "The first step to getting a handle on anything is expressing it to someone you trust—someone who won't judge you. I hear what you're saying and can tell you, more often than not, it comes up with others in your position. What you're telling yourself now is good for the psyche. Being in charge sometimes creates this feeling of accomplishment that is purely role based and not really who you are inside. It's easy to fall into thinking that absorbing every sling and arrow is mandatory and part of the deal."

He continued feeling that this was one of those teachable moments that Dan wasn't always open to. "Role dependency can sometimes become a creation of being successful in the eyes of others. What's most important is that you feel good about you. That is the reason the F^3 model addresses emotional independence in those areas that it does. Those around you, whether they are part of the family, the firm or your social networks, can inadvertently create a standard that can be impossible to live up to."

"Am I too far gone on this? Can I be happy if I step aside from FCI?"

Tom took a moment to reflect on Dan's questions. It was common for clients to need some encouragement. "That will depend entirely on finding purpose outside of this role, Dan. My thought is that you have every opportunity to make something work. The fact that you have a wide range of options available to you makes it easier in the end. That and the fact that you have demonstrated outside interests, like your cars and flying and recreational pursuits like golf. You may also find that freeing yourself up allows for more humanitarian pursuits."

With that the two men stood up.

"Okay, I'm looking forward to the business review and feeling better. I have to stop out at the hanger and look at the plane. Thanks, Tom."

The Firm

Fanny Fortune was in a hurry. Her father had called a few days prior and said that she and select others on the executive team were to attend a meeting with him, her mother and some advisors they were working with on the future of FCI. He had also directed her to Tibbs, who had arranged a meeting with Tom Coyle. Tom had given her a few questions to address about FCI. He directed her to bring her answers on flip-chart paper to the meeting with the rest of the group and be prepared to give her thoughts on how she saw the company. Now she wanted to get to the meeting with time to spare so she could get a prominent seat at the boardroom table.

Where the hell was Al, Fanny wondered?

Al was walking back toward the house, coming in from a meeting in the stable office with the farm veterinarian. He found himself a bit unfocused after receiving news from the vet that several of the stable's brood mares were coming to the end of their breeding years. Replacing them was something that, with the downturn in thoroughbred horseracing, needed to be thoughtfully considered. His mind was filled with the decision he faced and he didn't see Fanny backing her vehicle out of the garage and driving his way. She stopped, meeting him in the laneway, her car window rolling down as she rolled to a halt.

"Al, is your phone not on? I've asked you when you're on the property to carry a phone and have it on," she said. "Now the kids have a music recital on at school this afternoon and I'm not going to be able to make it again. You're up on this one."

Fortune's Impasse

Knowing that his day had just had a few wrinkles added to it, he nodded to his wife and said, "OK, I'm on it. Did they have a chance to practice this morning?"

She was already answering her cell, though, and through the tinted driver-side window she mouthed distinctly, "How would I know?" and drove slowly forward after a cross look back at her husband.

Jeff Fortune had now arrived at the GBA offices and was having a chat in the parking facility with RJ, who had driven her pickup over from an FCI location that had some operational issues. She knew that keeping the trust of those involved was paramount. Feedback was key, and she had covered some areas of strength and improvement with the location manager during a performance conversation early that morning.

She knew that the Fanny and Jeff feud was a challenge for all in leadership positions at FCI and thought she would mention how she was feeling about it. She knew it was wrong to side with either, but Fanny could be difficult. Jeff needed to step up, but not to the point of derailing the management team.

"So what are we in for today, RJ?" Jeff asked. "Something's up. Why isn't this meeting being held at the office?"

RJ considered what might lie ahead for all of them on this day. She certainly qualified in the group that would assemble as a "Day One-er." The "anchor," as Dan often called her, had seen massive changes since the days of the original Fortune Family Market, and she could scarcely believe it had happened quite the way it had.

RJ knew she shouldn't feel anything but admiration and affection for Dan and the Fortune family, but they'd been on a troubling path and it was tiring her out. She was, she felt, long past retirement and with the generous compensation she received, she really wasn't doing this for the money. She'd stayed single and was a model of fiscal prudence. The RJ Cameron scholarship was her pet project outside of the long hours she kept at FCI. It was a modest assistance plan conceived after a chance encounter with Ben Curtis at a CDC event. The scholarship directed funding toward promising women in MBA-level programs at the local college.

RJ carried weight within the industry on her own accord, as someone who had learned the business from the ground up. These days she was asked to speak at conferences and she enjoyed that very much. Dan was the face of FCI, but she knew that a call from her to anyone in the industry could get an immediate response when she needed one. She was tough but fair with FCI's suppliers and distributors, and they realized that a word from her to Dan Fortune could sway an opportunity both positively and negatively.

"Well, Jeff," she said, "I'm sure you did your homework for today? It'll be easy. Just call it as you see it."

Secretly, she wanted the best for Jeff, but she had a sense that things were evolving quickly and that he would need to assert himself. His older sister was also intent on moving FCI in her direction, and RJ knew that many in the company, if pressed, would admit to liking Fanny less, but trusting her more to keep the good ship FCI on an even keel in the future.

As they got into the elevator to go up to the GBA offices, RJ thought about Fanny and her own relationship with the dominant scion of the Fortune's next generation. Over the years, RJ had come to an unspoken understanding when it came to dealing with Fanny Fortune. She recalled the dustups that had occurred when Fanny had come to work for the family firm, especially the ones that involved her. She just couldn't seem to help herself.

In time, RJ had come to realize that both were strong women with high degrees of urgency when it came to the workplace. They were both very comfortable with confrontation. However, RJ felt she'd learned to avoid seeking it out, and to use that side of her only if it was absolutely required. Fanny was not similarly inclined.

Time after time, Fanny would let her emotions override her intelligence. It served to make her harder to work with if you didn't understand this about her. In getting things done through others, Fanny made mistakes of the head and not the heart. During the last few years, RJ had come to realize that Fanny was astute overall. She kept abreast of where FCI was at as a business and the market trends that defined its future.

When Jeff and RJ entered the room, it was alive with people from FCI talking and getting ready for the day. Marnie, who had come alone again, came over as the pair hung up their coats, and she greeted them warmly. "Dan promised he'll be with us in a few minutes. He called from his car and isn't far away."

Jeff saw that Fanny was sitting at the table already. He thought she looked slightly discomfited as she looked around from her chair. Scanning the room, he noted that the meeting table was circular, which meant everyone had a power seat, and he instantly felt that what they were all going to experience would be different and positive.

From their one-to-one meetings, the FCI people all knew Tom, and he now joined Marnie in walking Roger around the room to introduce him to everyone. Surprisingly, Roger already knew Bill Finch, FCI's CFO. Finch had attended a professional development forum where Roger had been part of a taxation panel that discussed leading strategies. Roger was pleased that Dan Fortune had a pro like Bill working on the FCI piece, as he'd thought the scenarios he raised in the panel discussion were pointedly accurate and well supported.

The last person from FCI was a younger man in, probably in his late twenties, Roger guessed. Derek Robb had been surprised to be invited. He was one of the new breed of location managers, and Dan knew he was the type the company wanted to hang on to. As Dan often told others at FCI corporate, his chance meeting with Derek was a real eye opener.

The day before meeting Derek for what he soon learned was the second time, he'd said to Tibbs and RJ in mock despair that he often thought that there hadn't been any great staff in the stores since he was the great staff in the store.

He noticed as he finished his offhand remark that RJ was giving him a sharp look and, knowing she'd been great too, he added, "Of course I meant us, RJ," and grinned.

As always, RJ picked her spot when it came to rising to a challenge. "Dan. Dan Fortune, you know we've been blessed with great people throughout the years and we paid dearly in those situations where we had the less than great. Underestimating the costs of having the wrong people was one of the largest financial drags in this company's history."

"When I'm in the stores I see all kinds of FCI staff that go out of their way to live up to the promises you make our customers in our advertising. If they were always breaking your promise, we wouldn't have the customer volumes we have. Would we?"

Dan was momentarily taken aback. His second in command was never one to hide her thoughts, and he felt badly at his off-the-cuff joke. He thought back to the day, long ago, when she'd rejected an inferior shipment of lettuce and told him that her goal—and what should be his—was to make it Fortune Family Markets with an "s" on the end.

"Get in your car and go see our manager at the Long Pond store. His name is Derek Robb, and he's one I have my eye on," she said. "This guy's monthly revenue and margin stats are through the roof. We have to clone him. He's that good."

Later that day, Dan found himself at the Long Pond store. He hadn't been there in quite a while, and intended to look up this Derek Robb. He'd visited the site over the years, but was unaware that there'd been a change in the location manager in the last year. As he wandered through unannounced, he was struck by the obvious age of the place: the antiquated shelving and refrigeration counters. This place is a project, he thought to himself, and made a mental note to look into its sales numbers to see if anything looked out of the norm. Why weren't they lagging, he wondered? This place could probably use some freshening up.

He was pleased, though, to see it all worked for those shoppers who were picking up a few late-day items. The staff was highly engaged in helping customers in the various departments, and he walked by one conversation in the floral department where a middle-aged man was being helped with a purchase of flowers. "Will you be taking these with you? Perhaps we can deliver them to your home or your wife's workplace, sir?" he heard the FCI associate ask.

The warmth of working people always trumps the fancy trappings of a futuristic location, he reminded himself.

He was momentarily transported to memories of the old Market store, his first. Dan had always focused staff on projecting the philosophy of the Market as a place that was customer friendly and easy to deal with. He'd kept the home delivery going as an added value to customers, even when the industry had abandoned the concept. Home delivery wasn't often requested now as people expected the immediacy of taking their shopping with them. He felt it was important to continue to offer it, though, especially to seniors.

When the Internet came along and with it the advent of online grocery shopping, FCI had established itself very early in that segment and incorporated it easily through its supply chain. It was really back to the future for them.

He was eased back into reality when he saw a young man eyeing him intently from the produce area. The fellow now advanced toward him.

"Sir, I hope you're finding everything you need, or perhaps I should say that are you finding everything here at Long Pond in order, Mr. Fortune?"

Dan smiled at the recognition.

"I should introduce myself. Derek Robb, sir. I am pleased to meet you again," the young manager said, realizing Dan didn't recall meeting him before.

"Yes, of course, Derek. It's been awhile, hasn't it?" Dan responded, searching for a reference point to their meeting. "How long has it been?"

"We met quite a few years back, right here, sir," Derek said to help Dan out and take away any vulnerability he might be feeling in not remembering. "You had come to visit the store. I was a recently hired part-time clerk and had been sent out to collect shopping carts in the back reaches of the parking lot.

"When I went out, I saw a man in a suit coming toward me, pushing a large train of carts from the far end of the lot with a huge smile on his face."

"And let me guess—that was me," Dan said, his mouth curving into the same broad grin. "I always tried to do that any time I went to a location, Derek. It grounded me, somehow—put me back to when I started out. You've been here ever since, Derek?"

Now the younger man had to pause as he reached out to straighten something askew at the end of a display. "No, sir. I am back here for a second time. I was here at this store through my teens and then I got an opportunity through the military to learn a skill and serve our country. My unit was deployed to the war zone toward the end of my second year. We were on the ground and in the middle of it by the end of our first month. It was an incredible change of scenery for all of us." Dan noticed that Derek's left hand was prosthetic. "Is that where you picked up that, Derek?" he said softly, not wanting to hear what he knew was inevitable.

"One day we were in an armored troop carrier going to an outer area to distribute medical supplies to the villagers. Part of the journey was in what we knew of as a 'hot zone.' Our TC vehicle hit an IED buried in the road. I was one of the lucky ones. Two in my unit didn't survive and those who did were all damaged in one way or the other. I was sent home and, after a stay in the veteran's hospital, was honorably discharged."

"I had enjoyed my time here and heard that FCI was a veteran-friendly company. Luckily, I was hired to work the night shift around five—no, six—years ago. Ms. Cameron heard about me and I got the opportunity to work my way up the ranks to where I am today."

Dan reached out and took Derek by both shoulders, "First, I want to thank you, son, for your sacrifice and that of your fellow soldiers. Our country owes you a debt we can't repay. And I'm glad you've come back to us and to FCI.

"Can you take some time to sit with me? Let's go to the café and get a coffee. It looks like I have a lot to learn from you, and I want to know your views on what we need to do in this store."

Strategic Thinking

Back at GBA that morning, the FCI group started to take their seats as Dan strode into the room and quietly took a place at the table, with a nod to those present.

Tom had been reviewing some of his notes from the one-to-one meetings he'd had with each person. He rose to his feet, looking around the room, and welcomed them all. As Roger had mentioned previously, Carrie would be unable to join them for this day as she was looking through the materials forwarded to GBA from all the Fortunes' professional advisors.

Tom started to speak. "Today, we'll get your views on FCI based on the questions you received when we met earlier. Let's consider ourselves to be in a laboratory. We have a chance today to talk about how each of you sees FCI, its potential and its challenges, at this point in time.

"First, let's be clear on the purpose and intention of whatever we do. Second, let's determine our comfort level and willingness to proceed.

"We have some simple objectives," he said, and he wrote them out on the whiteboard.

- Gain a better understanding of the company through each other
- Clarify how we see the business and marketplace today
- Create more time and space for ourselves and be prepared for the opportunity of advancing FCI in the future

"We can be informal. I'll be drawing straws so you all get a chance to make a presentation from the flip-chart papers you've brought with you.

My expectation is that you've read the questions and given thorough, honest feedback to everything we asked, as your views are vitally important. We're going to be open and free flowing."

Tom looked around, sensing that all were in agreement as he explained the thinking.

"It's fair and appropriate to explain different visions. We're not looking for the center of thought within this room but rather its farthest edge where you might push the envelope. These sessions get the best results when, if you feel the need, you add comments to your prepared notes. Something someone else says might trigger something you're thinking as well.

"Let's use 'back to the result' thinking. You've put a lot of work into your flip charts, I'm sure. So can we get started?"

Roger had approached the whiteboard as Tom spoke to the group and drew a scaled line underneath the words "THE FIRM." He also added two bullet points that were familiar to Dan and Marnie. These were

- Financial Strength and Resiliency
- Independence from the Founder

"Dan, would you like to say something to the group? If you would, tell us all what you're looking for today."

"Whatever happens, happens, but I need clarity," Dan said as he got up from the table, assuring the group of his own anticipation of a meaningful dialogue for them all. Dan now went to the whiteboard and wrote CLARITY. "It's important for me to listen and hear how you all see what we have here in contrast to my own views."

He pointed at a tube in the corner. "Those are my sheets; I'll be taking a turn as well, toward the end of the day, to give you all a chance to respond just to Tom's questions first."

Derek Robb now raised his hand tentatively. "Dan, I'd like to add something else to your list."

Dan glanced at Tom, wondering about the protocol of sessions like this. Who should be compiling this list? Tom motioned to him to continue. He knew engaging the room like this would ground Dan to the process even further. Besides, he thought, there were no real rules as to who got to hold the marker when creating an expectations list.

"OK, Derek, what would you like to see?" Dan asked, starting to get into the flow.

"I think we should write down ALIGNMENT, Dan. Whatever we see or say today is one thing, but I would hope we can come to mutual consensus and commitment to the fixes as an FCI team," Derek said.

Fanny had been looking around the room and thought she should weigh in with a request of her own before this process got away from her. "Dan, I would hope to hear how we all feel about our prospective staff requirements." She was pleased when Dan added FUTURE WORKFORCE to the list.

Jeff suggested ROLE DEFINITION. "I believe this is something we need to identify as important. I'm not sure how you're handling this in the stores," he said with a glance at Derek and RJ, "but we could use some attention to this elsewhere."

RJ asked that ACCOUNTABILITY be placed on the whiteboard. "I don't think that this subject ever gets spoken about too much."

Bill Finch put forward his expectation that all would be HONEST. "I know this goes without saying, but I'll say it anyway. What I mean by this is we can't say one thing and think another. This is too important and can potentially start us down the wrong path should we target the wrong areas."

Dan thought the group had compiled a reasonable list and was ready to hand the room back to Tom when he spotted Marnie raising her hand a little, not wanting to hijack the process. "I have two things that I believe should be on our list there, sir," she said to Dan.

"One is TRUST and the other is VALUES. I would like to see this group trust itself and our process today. 'Let's all leave our egos at the door' is a rather trite phrase, I think, but no one here has to be the smartest man or woman in the room."

Marnie was sensitive to saying too much, as she imagined that the others might not think she'd have a lot to say on the operational side of FCI, but she felt that a short reminder about values was also in order. She was thinking of her father and what he had said about value conflicts.

"I can also say that being judgmental isn't going to work. We need to appreciate and understand that others often see the world and FCI differently from the way we might. You may see something you vehemently reject, but let's give each other complete attention and then, reciprocally, you will get complete attention."

Dan now looked at his wife with a slight smile, wondering if her two suggestions were directed at him exclusively. He resolved to listen as well as he could and flipped the marker to Tom.

Throughout the day, Tom and Roger called upon the various attendees. One of the areas of inquiry was based on their views of the current status of FCI.

Each member of the group gave his or her individual perspectives on the following questions: How would you describe the current status of the business? What's working well in the business? What's not working so well? What needs changing? What are you personally good at? Not personally good at? What goes unspoken at FCI, but should be talked about?

They were also asked to address their own history and weave that into how they perceived FCI's past and their own place in it. Due to the varied ages and tenures with the group, there were very different perspectives on questions like, What have been the significant points in your personal career development path that have led you to here? How do you look back on your history?

After lunch, they went back to work and shared their varied visions concerning the future of FCI. This piece was particularly inspiring for Dan and Marnie. All spoke to the questions Tom had posited: Where do you see FCI in three to four years? What does the vision look like to you? Tom's advice on this section during the one-to-one sessions had been to be as specific as possible.

Finally, later in the day, Tom and Roger listened to the feedback from the group on how they would see FCI getting from where it was now to where it needed to go. This component addressed what each manager saw as the critical steps necessary to ensure that their vision was accomplished. Was it a number, a vision or a feeling? They were also asked to detail what they could foresee stopping or hindering them from achieving their desired outcome.

By the time each person had taken a turn at the front of the room, there were some tremendous insights, not only for Dan, but for the rest of the FCI team. They were excited at how their varying perspectives, coming from the different areas of the company, had some commonality.

It was also good for each to see where they differed. This didn't indicate a room in disarray, Tom noted, but a healthy conflict that was important to get through before it got lost in the mix of the day-to-day activity within the firm. Many of the ideas addressed would open other conversations on change that were important going forward and could be addressed later.

These differing views were most important to Dan and Marnie. They assessed the impact of what they were hearing on the succession plans that they were thinking about privately at that point.

Dan and Marnie had exchanged more than a few glances throughout the day. Both were amazed at the level of insight all had to offer. They were particularly gratified to see that both Fanny and Jeff were highly involved in the discussion, with much to say on the future of the firm.

One of the day's highlights was praise for the supply chain. As a group, they felt the FCI systems of procurement and distribution were particularly well thought out and working well. RJ noted that Jeff's contribution to equipment design in the distribution center allowed the supply chain to deliver fresher products to the stores, faster than ever before. This cut down on the need for constant counter culling of decaying produce. The result was measurably lower labor costs and higher in-store margins. Jeff was pleased and made note to get this feedback out to others on the supply chain team.

As RJ went on to note, this wasn't a case of the company wheels being ready to fall off. When she got to her segment on the future, everyone in the room laughed when she drew a quick picture that portrayed someone gardening with a sunhat on. "I have to retire soon, people. You will not have to call in a taxidermist to make sure I hang in there forever. Dan, you might consider following my lead!"

The main points from the group input in this area were telling. Not everything was running perfectly and all raised points of concern as well. Bill Finch noted the lack of business acumen of some of the key people. "They are good people and my thought is that those who find themselves attracted to our business tend to be people oriented. I think they fall into it while searching for something else and then some like it and stay. The next thing they know, they've hung in for such a significant part of their lives that they become our core employees.

"I still think we're missing some potential because our workforce lacks a better understanding of the business model. Do they understand our profit picture and how their personal activities either add to profits or let cash slip through the cracks day to day? Do they benefit directly enough to care?"

Bill was raising an issue that Dan had never felt fully comfortable addressing. Like many companies, FCI had a bonus system, which in effect was an additional stipend at the end of the year. Most who received it felt it was part of the pay packet and counted on it to look after holiday season bills or perhaps a winter getaway.

The problem for Bill was that he felt most recipients didn't associate the extra money with job performance, but more as a gift from Dan personally. The two men had discussed it over the years, and Dan wasn't surprised to hear Bill bring it up now.

"I think we ought to open our thinking on profit-based compensation," he said, looking at Dan for acknowledgement.

Derek's countered the CFO's comment, and his input raised some eyebrows. "Yes, but do we want a group of wannabe accountants dealing with our most prized resource, our customers? I would like to cut down our staff turnover at a store level. Sifting through those people who find their way to us and then hoping a certain percentage stay is an expensive way to build our bench strength," Derek said, demonstrating observational qualities that RJ found unique.

Despite knowing he might be a bit out on a limb with the CFO, he stayed with his point. "That's what I think, Bill," the young manager stated. "Isn't what we're really selling our consumer is a sense of the ideals that the Fortune Family Market had, once Mr. Fortune here took it on? You know, 'Simple family fare from simpler times'?"

Bill took in the comment with a nod and said, "I think there's room for that core ideal to be married with a workforce that's more astute and tuned into the financial measures that are in place for the broader company, Derek. I don't have a problem with us changing our recruiting philosophy, and perhaps it does have to be updated. Should we go down that route, I think we all agree a metric has to be placed on changing our ways of bringing new people on board. Is going with a different philosophy going to make a measurable difference for the money it will cost?"

"How are you measuring the current way of doing things?" Derek asked, causing a moment of reflection to encompass them all.

After a long pause, Bill gave a slight laugh. "Well you have me there. I don't think we do," he said, glancing toward the ceiling in thought as he spoke. He then turned toward RJ, his eyes wide but with a smile, and mouthed, "Where'd you get him from?"

Fanny and Jeff

Fanny's contribution that afternoon was particularly insightful. Her expertise shone through as she addressed the demographics upon which FCI had been founded and the shifts that were occurring. For some time, she'd felt these demographics needed to be addressed in their marketing strategy.

"I'll start my feedback by saying we're not going to, nor should we, go 'down market' in our search for customers."

She spoke in a louder voice than the others, but commanded the room with more than just her volume. Fanny had her father's magnetism. Dan and Marnie had long known that others would listen to her as long as they didn't feel beaten down in the process.

"We should not go down market for the discount customer. My data tells me we're extremely well placed," she repeated. "A survey we commissioned in the last quarter told us that the average grocery shopper sees us as part of the family and not necessarily a stop-and-grab transactional business. In essence, FCI is a strategic partner to them as they live their lives and raise their families. When they suffer losses or experience life's victories and special events, FCI is there for them. With Dan at the helm, we have transcended into a lifestyle brand. That media campaign that we featured over the years has worked."

Fanny had taken her mother's expectation to heart and hadn't had too many tangles with the others on their presentations, other than to make careful notes and ask the odd clarifying question for context on certain points that others brought up.

Later in her presentation, she talked about the future consumer being as interested in a fresh, locally produced product—whether that purchase came from the meat, seafood or produce department, or from the in-store bakeries—as they were in the price.

She also noted that customers were expressing their preference for innovation in what many thought of as a staid, mature industry. Keeping this segment engaged with new strategies—such customer-friendly concepts as cooking schools, nutrition advice and social media groups—was key. She told the group of a marketing concept that would enable FCI to direct message customers that opted in to receive daily social media messaging. For example, a message could be sent on what was currently available from the store's hot food counters. Customizing the customer experience would be paying off in the years ahead.

"We all know that the dinner options at the takeout counters change by the hour as we run out of available product. We have diminishing product through the hours of 4 to 9 p.m., when people are trying to put dinner together. We could broadcast a discount on overages we have in our counters. We'd reduce waste and be able to measure the accuracy for our customer's menu likes and dislikes by area.

"This will lead to better information for our kitchen managers on what sells and what doesn't. Even seasonal disparity will be measurable," Fanny explained.

"I also want to note that the new stuff Jeff is doing on the supply side is showing up in my consumer data. Our perceived freshness numbers have never charted as high since I've been involved with the company. I'd like to recognize you, Jeff, for your contribution.

"In distribution, we have a special weapon that at this point no one else can match; so exploiting it is where we should go."

Jeff looked down at his notes as Fanny praised his work. It was unexpected, as they hadn't communicated at all in the last few months. His team communicated with Fanny's office on matters that were germane to FCI and, otherwise, they'd had no personal contact.

Fanny finished up her presentation, following Tom's suggested template, with her thoughts on other areas of FCI. She succinctly addressed the areas she thought would hold them back from getting to the place she'd painted in her future vision segment. "No guts, no initiative, no execution" was all she'd written.

RJ and Derek questioned Fanny on that last point before she sat down.

"Fanny, it appears you're pretty sure on your analytics. It all looks good. Can you show some supporting documentation?" RJ asked.

Before Fanny could address RJ, Derek jumped in with another question. "Fanny, I like what you said. I couldn't agree more that we have to press home the advantages we have. Have you considered the right way to address this at a store level? I think most location managers will be worried about the logistics and their own comfort with technology."

Fanny left the group with the impression that there was a bright future for the company and everyone in the room felt good about what they had heard. Her presentation created a buzz with the others and she concluded her time at the front with answers for both RJ and Derek.

"I was going to release a report on what I've said here today, but decided to hold it until I ran the concept by this group, as I need your feedback and then assistance in implementing it," she explained. "This session and listening to you all is telling me that I should go back and change it. This process has taught me that things that I thought were obvious aren't.

"I'm going to create a new document that will lay out what I'm thinking. It will incorporate the feedback from this meeting and provide the supporting data we need as well as an overview for the stores," Fanny answered as she sat down.

Dan and Marnie looked at each other, thinking the same thing. Both could count on one hand the times in Fanny's life that she would admit to being taught anything.

Jeff now unfolded his presentation and started to explain his views on the business.

He took the group through areas that he thought were good and bad about FCI. He mentioned what he considered to be his own strengths and then covered what he felt he would like to improve in himself. Marnie took some notice that Jeff described himself as coming at most problems from the compromised perspective of an empathetic engineer.

"It's incongruous—an oxymoron for a person in my field. I've been trained to be black and white in my approach to problems, but I have this inner dichotomy of being a people person. I wasn't like most of my classmates in school. Frankly, I see it as something that weakens me."

"Nonsense," Dan said quietly, thinking back to Double F. "You don't need to change yourself, Jeff."

His entry point into the firm was covered in his history and was something that allowed Jeff to explain himself, his background, his memories and why he came to work. In the end, Jeff gave a heartfelt explanation of his feelings about FCI and what it all meant to him personally.

Tom had found that asking people to talk about their past and how they got involved in their career and the company was critical. It allowed them to humanize themselves to each other. This was a fairly cohesive group, and they felt they knew each other well. However, as with many client groups, there were moments of surprise as people disclosed information about their backgrounds, their educations and their own families.

Jeff continued outlining his own vision, which was principally focused on his side of the business and what the supply chain might look like in years to come, and then he addressed the potential issues he could see keeping FCI from reaching its goals.

"I want to tell you about challenges and what the template described as holdbacks, but I think I can address those by telling you what I feel goes unspoken around here," he told them.

Both Dan and Marnie drew in a breath, sensing that the dam was going to burst on all the goodwill the group had experienced so far in the day.

"It's simple, really. My mother addressed it earlier. It's trust. Do we trust each other? Do we trust FCI's project teams and staff? Do they trust us?" Jeff paused for a drink of water and then continued. "Do we trust each other?"

"I don't think anything we've said today on the future of FCI stands a chance without trust and less of the second-guessing I've experienced lately."

When Jeff spoke, Fanny sat back in her chair and looked at Dan as if asking for him to intervene, but Dan stayed out of it, remembering his opening comment of whatever happens happens.

Jeff continued. "I guess it is appropriate to say here that this is really between Fanny and me."

Fanny attempted to dissuade Jeff from continuing. "Jeff does this make sense here, in a planning exercise?"

"This isn't a planning exercise; it's an opportunity for us all to speak on where we see the firm right now. It didn't say it specifically on Tom's template, but I took it as implied, that we discuss warts and all," he shot back.

"I can say that I felt very hurt, Fanny, when I heard what you did out at the plant when there were rumors of changes to health inspections and that we weren't ready. We were and still are ready. You had no business and no authority to be out there doing that. If you wish to be the point person for an FCI political strategy, great. We all know you have the network to influence on our behalf. However, that doesn't warrant going over anyone's head. I should have been called on that first.

"I said earlier that my main objective was to get some better understanding of my role because, obviously, it isn't what I thought it was."

Fanny looked around, trying to compose herself in the midst of the upbraiding from Jeff. "Well, I'm sure you've waited awhile to say that, haven't you, brother?" she spat, her own fire starting to light.

Dan made a move to get to his feet to end it, embarrassed to have the family laundry aired in front of the others. Marnie held her arm firmly over his and motioned with her eyes to let it play out. "This is a business, Dan; these things happen," she whispered.

RJ turned to face Dan. "Boss, this needs to be settled, as it has the potential to cause more damage than it already has."

Dan looked over at Roger and Tom to see if they were taking it in. Both were watching to see how the group would take this turn of events.

Derek motioned to Tom that he wished to speak. "I don't have near the experience that the rest of you have in this business, but I do have experience being in firefights that often have tragic consequences. Not only for those involved, but collateral damage for those that aren't. I can tell you that smart people not directly involved run away when something like that breaks out."

RJ addressed the room. "The word in the industry is that FCI people are being called on job openings with our competition. Where do we go if this can't be solved, folks?"

Derek absentmindedly rubbed the thumb of his prosthetic hand while he spoke. "I can also tell you that the people that are directly involved should avoid it as well and never get something like that started in the first place. Long-term conflicts have very few good purposes. Out in the world or inside places like this."

He continued to express himself, even though he felt like he was walking through a minefield. "Based on what we've heard from each other today, it would be a shame to not try and figure out what to do here. It's obvious that we aren't perfect and we're beating ourselves up a little here, but there's more good here than bad, isn't there?"

Dan saw his moment to enter the conversation and jumped to his feet, avoiding Marnie's hand trying to anchor him to his chair.

"Okay, guys. Let's get back to what we came here to do today," he said. Over the next 45 minutes he told them all how he saw the business. He repeated almost verbatim what he'd told Tom, Roger and Carrie in previous days leading up to this day's meeting, but shaped his comments around the template that the rest of the group worked from.

As far as FCI's stability was concerned, he agreed that FCI was in reasonable shape but more vulnerable if some of the areas that had been pointed out were not addressed. Frankly, he admitted that some of the problems were a bit worse than he'd previously thought.

He closed off his contribution to the session by likening what he was hearing to a plumbing problem, where the businesses pipes were clogged due to the maturity of the business. The other clogs came from people not being on the same page. If these clogs weren't cleared soon, together, they would affect the three key pieces of FCI's valuation: its customers, its products and its people.

It had been a long day and, while the issues that Fanny and Jeff had had with each other weren't solved, at least it had been a chance to point out the unspoken conflict of which many in the company were painfully aware.

Tom came up to the front to ask the group to identify the main points coming out of the day. "Can you tell me what jumps out at you from today? What should you tackle in the future?"

He wrote them out on the whiteboard and noted the name of the person who volunteered the point for future follow up:

- A metrics-based human resources plan for improving finding, focusing and keeping FCI personnel—Bill
- Regular sessions away from the workplace for the executive team and unit teams to discuss issues. (Stamp out the sparks before they become forest fires, become better at prevention.)—RJ
- Implement Fanny's food counter ideas at a store level—Derek
- Establish an agreed-upon set of FCI core values—Marnie
- Role alignment and clarity (first at an executive level)—Jeff
- Strategic planning—Fanny

After a few edits, Tom stepped back from the list. He hadn't asked for any prioritization of the list yet. And no one had questioned that Dan hadn't made any suggestions.

Roger joined Tom at the front of the room.

Directing his attention to the FCI people, he asked them to be as objective as possible and to write down a number between 0 and 10 to address where they felt the company was on the two central issues. The first question was: How independent is FCI from Dan and the shadow he casts over the company, within the industry, with FCI supplier and customer relationships?

On this question, Tom explained that a score of 10 reflected an FCI where Dan was not needed to set the direction of the company. A high score would acknowledge that Dan's influence with commercial and social relationships within the industry and suppliers had been fully transferred from himself to others within the company. Was FCI a bird that had left the nest and taken wing, now able to navigate without its founder?

In contrast, a score nearer 0 showed a company that was very dependent on the control that the founder still needed to exert on a day-to-day basis within the firm. This control was extended to all or most external relationships. The FCI brand and Dan Fortune could be considered one and the same.

Roger addressed the second question with the group. He asked what their sense of FCI's financial strength and resiliency was. Roger cautioned them to forget about all the personalities involved; instead, the perspective here was what if this was a competitor—a rival company that FCI was looking at acquiring? How would you view the company?

"Try to take your own emotional attachment out of the way you rank FCI, and find a number," he said. "It's not so much your accuracy but rather how the group feels about the answer."

Roger advised that a higher score reflected a firm that had a strong balance sheet, strong and growing profits, growing and diversifying markets, solid and growing market share and proven and stable leadership.

Based on what they had discussed, the group settled on a 6, which was slightly lower than Dan had given the same scale in one of the lead-up meetings. Sifting through what he'd heard, he was content to lower his own score of 7. After all, he rationalized, they had a better handle on the day to day. He was glad they didn't see it as a complete mess, though.

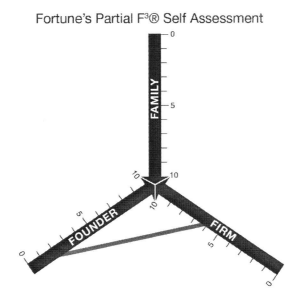

Fortune's Partial F³® Self Assessment

The reason for the 6 was that, even with Dan at the helm, the group had wrestled with readiness of the executive team to take advantage of the potential of FCI. The individual ratings diverged widely amongst the group, with Fanny rating this factor as an 8 and everyone else rating it as a 5 or a 6.

Fanny looked around her while the group debated this issue. "Why," she wondered, "would they ever take a shot at themselves?"

It struck her as a bit treasonous, especially with her father in the room. Didn't they know what he had gone through to create what they all were charged with leading?

She now raised her hand and said, "What's the big deal, Tom? Roger? Are we in trouble? Because if we are, I certainly don't see it. Some of these issues have evolved over an extended period of time, but we have soldiered on as a company. There won't be any immediate fixes.

"And, let's not all forget that FCI has historically been profitable and still is," she reminded them. "We make money—" Fanny repeated for emphasis. "My data says we have some good things going on. Don't we all see what I am seeing?"

As Tom started to reply, Dan stood up to answer a question he considered more properly addressed to him, and with a sigh, began to speak. "We believe there's a window here for fulsome conversation on the future, a future that will not include me in an operational role at FCI. I will not be around forever."

There was an audible gasp from RJ, and Marnie couldn't help but notice the raised eyebrows and jaw dropping from both Fanny and Jeff.

Dan, noticing the look of concern in the group, raised both his hands in an attempt to calm the room. "This isn't health related, not this time, anyway. Marnie and I have been working with Roger and Tom. Also Carrie, who you may have seen in the outer office through the breaks we've had today or on your way in. They've all been helping us get a handle on our financial future and the family, and this includes turning our attention to developing and implementing a management succession plan for FCI."

Jeff spoke up, saying, "Dad, this is a bit of a shock. Why now? Are you sure about this?"

"Sure about what?" Dan asked, pointedly avoiding his son's eyes.

"Well, about us having to carry on without you day to day. That would be a huge change for all of us and this is coming at us out of the blue. For me, anyway," he said with a quick glance at Fanny, who he felt seemed slightly disengaged, as though she wasn't listening to the exchange between him and his father.

Now taking in the whole table, Dan said, "Well, actually, I'm not sure what I want to do yet and how fast this will proceed, but I do know that I'm not getting any younger. There are many issues involved in this type of transition, some personal, some that affect our family and all that affect FCI and the people in this room. Marnie and I have agreed that we would like to deal with this while time is our friend and we have as many options as possible."

"Yes, this is a bit of a surprise." said Fanny in disbelief, now coming out of her daze. "Who will replace you?" she added quickly.

"The people at GBA have helped us, or more accurately me, realize that this issue is to be dealt with for the benefit of FCI and our family," replied Dan, slowly trying to think of how to respond to the question.

"Through the process that the GBA team is leading us through, we will be able to determine what that transition will look like," Marnie added, seeing that Dan was flagging some in his explanation and knowing that he was still uncomfortable with the thought of stepping back, let alone out.

"I didn't want to tell any of you before today," he said, now looking at both his children as he spoke. "Well, certainly not prior to your preparations for this session here, anyway.

"While the succession issue is primarily ours," Dan said, pointing to himself and Marnie, "we wanted to get a read on where all of you see FCI at this point in time and how you collectively see its future.

"In experiencing your presentations, I'm pleased with the result here today. That's not to say that you haven't surprised me. You each raised issues that were real insights to me and that I wouldn't have understood. Marnie and I would like to thank all of you for your thoughtful and honest input."

Tom sensed a feeling of collective vulnerability in the room. The call to action had to come from within, he knew. The pieces they'd identified were their priorities and not handed to them by an outsider.

In reviews like this, once participants had each been given a chance to speak, they could all see where they were aligned and where they might differ. The first step in implementing any change was the group's admission and understanding of a common cause and the realization that they could see the same things. The FCI group had listed the main issues, but they were all larger themes that would need to be thoughtfully and carefully addressed. Plans to improve in areas where issues had been raised would be the next step, once the final pieces of the Fortune transition were clear.

The meeting was ended and those from FCI left the GBA offices, except for Jeff, who stayed behind to talk with Tom and Roger.

"Guys, this was a shocker. I just want Dad to be happy. It will be quite a change for him. He was bagging groceries at the original Market when he was eight. It's engrained in him as it can possibly be. That said, I'm wondering where we should go with this."

"We're going to meet with you as a family, Jeff." Roger said. "After that, it should become clearer. By using F^3 and showing all of you the full model, we can then have the right kind of conversation about FCI's leadership succession options and how all of you in the next generation can fit into that. This is an opportunity that, much like today, gives all of you the opportunity and tools to shape what things can look like in the future."

Jeff walked out to his car and noticed that Fanny had her vehicle idling. He assumed she was making a few calls before hitting the highway to get home. He was stepping into his car when he heard her passenger power window sliding down and could hear some muffled sobs emanating from the interior of the truck.

He shut his door and went over to look in on his sister, who had her hand over her eyes. "Jeff, can you get in for a minute? We need to talk.

"I'm so upset by what went down just now and I can't just drive home like nothing happened. A few years back when Dad was sick I asked myself, what if the worst happened. I never dreamed that he couldn't pull through that, though, and when he did I just thought it was business as usual.

"Jeff, I think you know this, but if not, I have to level with you right now. I've always dreamed of succeeding him, but I am not sure I'm ready. What can we do to convince him to stay?"

Jeff replied after considering his own emotions with Fanny's disclosure. It had been clear to him for some time that Fanny was gunning for more authority within FCI. Her actions said as much.

"I think an outsider would tell us both that we're not ready, Fanny. If there was only one of us and not two, there would be pieces to add to our fitness for the president role that we may lack now. We can't convince him to stay. I suspect that this is the hardest decision he's ever considered making and he's made some big ones, taken big gambles …"

"What if he's thinking about selling it, though, Jeff? That scares me. What would he do? What would I do? What would you do? You know how these things go down. Someone else buys in and the old guard gets thrown out like day-old donuts," Fanny said, wincing. "I can't have that. I can't imagine an FCI without our family involved," she said, a tone of conviction in her voice that Jeff had heard time and again.

"He didn't say he wanted to sell, but if he did, there's nothing stopping you from buying it," Jeff said.

"Nor you," she quickly shot back.

At this exchange, they both stared at the windshield for a moment, reflecting on what that kind of commitment meant to either of them. Fanny punched the steering wheel and they both started to laugh.

"Do you know how freakin' hard it would be to put that kind of money together, to take that kind of gamble for either of us?" Fanny nearly screamed, "I like my life just the way it is."

Jeff's laughter came to an end with a sobering thought of his own." Yeah, Fan, but in the long term, they're not going to live forever and neither are you and I. We have to think of our own children, the third generation. We have this lovely problem that many people would like to be faced with. Don't we?

"I think we're getting way ahead of ourselves and we need to see Dad and Mom's options. I want them to be happy. If we could get them set up similar to what the Curtises did, then I think that would work. It may not turn out that way, but we have to let them have a chance," Jeff said. "I know they also have to consider what would be fair to Inge and Jimmy. They have a part to play in this, too. We're meeting as a family next week. Let's see where that goes.

"I hung back with Tom and Roger after the meeting, before coming out here. Roger was explaining that this is just the start of the process. Transition plans can take a while to unfold. Using their F^3 model creates a picture for us. It helps to get everyone's perspective on the table and helps us identify what's possible for everyone involved. Once it's complete and everyone understands it."

"Jeff, you're made for this type of stuff. I don't think I am," Fanny said, still not seeing that this could be anything but damaging. "Collective thinking has never been me. I just get things done and don't wait around for a lot of opinions."

"I don't know about that. You were the star of the show in there today. I didn't like what you did to me at the plant, but from what I saw, you knew your stuff cold on your presentation. It would be a big loss to FCI, whatever happens, if they lost you," Jeff said.

"The fact that I don't wait around for consensus has also been one of my major weaknesses. Sorry. You were right—I should have gone to you. Some days I just can't help myself," came her reply.

Inge and Jimmy Explain

Dan looked into his dressing closet mirror and thought of the day ahead. He had dressed in his usual uniform—a navy suit and white shirt—and was now searching out a particular tie that he favored. Where was that red striped tie, he wondered?

For him it was a monumental day, but one that was not without some trepidation on his part. With all that had been done to this point, he didn't feel he had a good grasp on the critical area of the Fortune family itself. With all his children quite reliant on him in one way or another, he saw advantages in maintaining the current situation. He and Marnie couldn't live with losing control and having them devolve into more conflict with each other.

A few minutes later he went down to the breakfast room where Marnie was already back from her daily brisk walk. Her route was fairly fixed: past the stables and out through the grazing pastures. She would never miss her walk unless the weather was terrible, and terrible to her was a gale-force storm. She was reading the newspaper, seemingly quite unaffected by what the day might bring them both.

Each of the next generation of Fortunes had had an individual meeting with the GBA people over the previous few days. Inge and Jimmy were introduced to the F^3 model and were asked about their own perspectives. They discussed how they identified with FCI and the relationship each had with his or her parents and the rest of their siblings.

Both Inge and Jimmy were circumspect when it came to FCI. Neither saw the family firm as the vehicle in which they wished to pursue careers. FCI was, as Inge put it, a means to an end.

"Don't we all just want to live a life of purpose?" she asked the GBA team during her individual meeting. "I've had my bad moments, but I'm still happy with my direction. I think my contribution of my time to noteworthy causes like the art gallery is worthwhile. Participating in the fundraising is hard work but seeing the end result is really fulfilling."

It appeared to Roger and Carrie that Inge was at least emotionally independent of FCI. She pursued her own interests and didn't identify with the family firm other than as a place to buy her own groceries.

"I can walk through most of the locations in this city and no one that works there would know who I am. Sure, I run into friends and people that know me from my obligations with the art community, but I see no reason to announce myself. As a customer, I think they have great stores, but other than that, I'm just one of the public when I go," Inge explained.

Inge was more tentative about her financial independency and was at a loss to explain whether she felt a real reliance on the business.

"I live what I believe is a fairly austere existence. I think I get that from being surrounded by art all day. An artist, in many cases, creates from nothing other than the resources available at the time of a creative inspiration. I try to emulate that day to day.

"Sure, now looking back at when I was married, my life was one of excess. My husband spent a lot of money and liked to live life as he put it at 'the top of the mountain.' My father and mother rescued me from a bad situation and, as you may know, Alfie was paid very well to leave," Inge explained, with a subconscious shrug.

"So if you're asking whether I need money from the family, the answer is yes and no. I do fund my living expenses through regular disbursements from a trust my father established for us. I do own my own condo at Harborside, and it's mortgage free. I am debt free other than cards that I clear monthly. I do manage to save some of my trust money. As I receive it, I channel a good portion into my own investment fund, independent of my family."

"What do you think you'll use that money for?" Roger asked.

Inge thought for a moment before answering, and then, feeling comfortable enough to disclose a small secret, opened up on this area of her life. "Well, my feeling is that there are many artists around who are working outside of the mainstream but still creating worthy pieces. These people need to be supported and, while I don't consider myself to be a benefactor or a sponsor for them, let's say I help with the groceries now and again. I will get my payback from some as they develop. My father would go mad if he knew this was happening, but I feel it's my own money, and when I give some away I do without something else."

Without full disclosure of Dan's transition options, Roger felt it would help Inge to better understand if she thought ahead to some kind of ownership in FCI. He detailed a scenario where some of her siblings might remain in operational roles, but also join her as a shareholder.

"As you have heard, I have no interest in working there, but being a shareholder would be a different story," she admitted, visibly brightening at the prospect of such a role.

"What I really want to do is provide a family orientation to the work our foundation could do. We need to connect my father to what is required. I would like to formalize my own position as a managing director, but we are going to need to add some paid positions for staff. My own role will be unpaid; I would rather direct that amount back into the foundation."

After Inge left, there was a break of 30 minutes before Jimmy Fortune's arrival. Carrie and Roger were in the middle of breaking down Inge's feedback for the eventual customization of the meeting agenda for the family meeting later in the week, when Tom poked his head into Rogers's office.

Roger asked, "Tom, are you going to be able to join us for the meeting with Jimmy Fortune? He's expected here quite soon."

Tom nodded. "I certainly will. Dan told me Jimmy is considering a start-up of his own. Dan asked me for an opinion on the concept and to give Jimmy some feedback on what I thought. I need to ask Nikki to look out for a courier, but I will be back."

Tom was bent down giving Higgins a scratch behind the ear when the door chime signaled someone entering. He appraised a young man entering the reception area. Lightly built and garbed in a cycling shirt and shorts, he had long hair, a full beard, piercing green eyes and a shy smile. Tom wondered if this might be his bike courier who was picking up the parcel for him.

Before Tom could ask him who he was looking for, the young man spoke.

"Are you Mr. Mason?"

"No, but Roger is just down the hall," he said. He turned to move and then stopped short when the visitor identified himself.

"Can you tell him that Jim Fortune is here? I have a meeting with him. I'm a little early, I think."

Before turning back to Jimmy, Tom thought, Wow, what a family. Everyone has his or her own style. "Jim, is it? I'm Tom Coyle. I'm pleased to meet you. I'll be sitting in with you today as well. Please make yourself comfortable and we'll bring you in shortly."

"Yes, my father told me about you, Mr. Coyle. It's nice to meet you as well."

Tom went on down the hall to inform the others.

The youngest Fortune looked around the reception area, somewhat ill at ease thinking about what he might say to his parents' advisors. Just then, Higgins came in to the room to greet the new arrival. Jimmy reached into his pocket while petting Higgins, saying that he'd heard all about him. He dug out a package of biscuits and offered a piece to the friendly dog. "Yes, pal, I've heard all about you, too."

"I see you've made a friend, Higgins," Carrie said as she came out to bring Jimmy into the meeting. "Just don't be bothering our visitor all afternoon." She introduced herself and they both went back to see Roger and Tom.

In Roger's office, Tom introduced Jimmy to Roger, and the group started to cover the questions that would allow Jimmy to identify where he saw himself in the Fortune family puzzle.

Jimmy started with a short overview of his own background, without reference to any of the recent troubles he'd had with the law.

"My path has been different," he said, his eyes searching the skyline out Roger's window as he launched into a short overview. "I've never had much of a connection to FCI. I think that Dad, Fanny and Jeff have things well in hand over there. I just wouldn't fit in.

"I can tell you that I haven't even been in a store in years. When I was in high school, I used to bring in some friends at lunch hour and occasionally after school. I had some trouble when a few of the kids were caught shoplifting and they called Dad. He was pissed off but he got over it.

"It was a mistake and it was wrong, but in the end I just stopped going in there. To me, the place was more trouble than it was worth. Even in the last years when I was on my own, I just went through the alley to the farmer's market the odd time or to the Quickie Mart at the gas station for food, but mostly ate out," Jimmy explained.

"How do you provide for yourself?" Carrie asked.

"Well ..." Jimmy let out a sigh. "I don't have a lot of expenses. I've given up my place downtown and moved into the guest house at my parents'. I guess I'm a young country squire these days," he said, laughing, but clearly some sadness and embarrassment crowded into his voice.

"I love being with my father and my mother, too, actually. I'm trying to get myself together at this point. I've got some ideas and want to do it right. "

Was he provided with any money, Roger wondered? Roger knew that no distributions were being made to Jimmy from the trust fund. Dan had previously set up the trust to start providing funding at the age of thirty, and Jimmy, Roger knew, was still a few years away.

It was a good thing, too, he realized. Jimmy needed to choose his direction himself, not at the behest of his parents, but with conditions on assistance. "So what now, then?" Roger asked on behalf of all three of them, noticing that Carrie had stopped writing and Tom was in full pause, waiting to see where the story went.

Sensing that he had an audience and needing to add to their understanding of him, Jimmy continued. "Dad gives me an allowance of sorts and I receive it pretty much every Friday."

"Pretty much?" Carrie said.

Jimmy smiled. "Well if you know Dan Fortune, you know that he isn't above turning off the tap when he becomes unhappy about something. From time to time, he has felt he had a few reasons to be unhappy, I guess."

Tom, sensing that a change of gears was necessary, asked Jimmy, "What is it that you're really interested in?"

"Anything vintage," was Jimmy's ready reply. "Old cars, boats. Cedar strips mostly. Then there are planes, motorcycles … you name it. There's a ton of money spent on this stuff, and I grew up around it. My dad and I are both interested."

"Is this something you would like to become involved in?" Tom said, pursuing this thought. "As a business or still as a hobby? What's your background on the trade ticket required?"

"As a business, of course. As far as obtaining a license, I'm halfway there and would like to continue my education to get it. However, my plan is to get more into the buy, restoration and sell business. I've talked to my father about funding a start-up where I would bring in another person as the back shop guy at first. I could be front counter and help with some of the small stuff. I would only want my license for the credibility and knowhow, but if it's going to be a business, I would need to keep my focus on the prospects and customers.

"Who knows, maybe we could develop a TV show around some of the restorations of the rare pieces we get our hands on," Jimmy explained, getting more animated as he thought of the possibilities.

"So it sounds, then, as though an active role in FCI is not currently in your plans?" Roger asked.

"Not a chance," was Jimmy's succinct response.

"How about in a shareholder's role in the future, perhaps in partnership with your brother and sisters?" Carrie questioned, noticing that Higgins had chosen that moment to stick his head through the office door.

"You have a super dog. What breeder did you get him from? I know what he wants. You're wondering if I have any treats, aren't you, pal?" Jimmy said, once again digging into his pocket. After a few seconds with Higgins, he was ready to re-engage the group on Carrie's question. "Well, let's face it—my parents have a lot of resources. My problem is I have less than a neutral relationship with FCI. Frankly, I can't stand the place. If my father wanted to fund me and provide some seed money, I would rather do that.

"Fanny's the one who lives it and breathes it. Jeff loves the company, too, but in a different way. Jennifer, his wife—she's a Curtis, you know," he told them with a slightly conspiratorial tone. "She keeps him pretty grounded. He's the best brother a guy could have, but we're never going to be close.

"Inge is Inge. Dad once called her a silk stocking socialist. I don't even know what that means. All I know is that if you can come up with something really crazy and call it art, she'll be all over it and want to hand you some of Dad's money," Jimmy mused, still petting Higgins as he spoke.

"I grew up an only child. I'm sure I was cute and all that at first, but they went off to school very early in my life and then came back. We never did connect after that. I was just a screw-up in their eyes, and to me they were always doing things I couldn't do and going places I couldn't go.

"No, I love them all, but I don't think I want to be business partners," Jimmy Fortune concluded.

The Family Weighs In

Nikki Kingsmill was the first in to the GBA office the morning of the Fortune family meeting. As the elevator rose, she began thinking about setting things up for the group. As she understood it, Roger, Tom and Carrie would all be in, and they would be hosting Mr. and Mrs. Fortune; their daughter and son-in-law, Fanny and Al; Jeff Fortune and his wife Jennifer; Inge and the youngest, Jimmy. Carrie had sent her an email the previous day to say that Jimmy would now be known as Jim, but she didn't know why.

There was a subtle sway, and the chime signified that it was her floor. She stepped out, noting that someone in the hall ahead of her had disappeared through the men's room door. Just another tenant, she thought, unlocking the doors at GBA.

She busied herself with the preparations for the meeting, as it would be starting in just over an hour. She heard a chime in the reception area and wondered which of her three office mates had arrived. She called out to whoever was there, "Good morning."

A young man appeared at the entrance of the meeting room. "Am I the first one here?"

Slightly startled to see someone else so early, she collected her thoughts and said, "You must be Jimmy; I mean Jim Fortune? I'm Nikki, and I'm pleased to meet you. Can I get your coat and offer you a coffee?" she asked.

"No, no," Jim said, waving her off. "I was here the other day and we didn't meet, but I know where the closet is. I'll have a coffee, but later. I'll wait for everyone else." He left the room to hang up his coat and was soon back.

251

"Well, Jim, make yourself comfortable. You may have messages to check? I'm just setting up for today's session."

He was slightly taken aback by her assumption that he might have anything going on that required that level of immediacy. "Messages." Jim smiled bashfully. "No, Nikki, no one's looking for me this early. I'd like to help you, though. What can I do?"

Sensing that telling him she had it taken care of might be perceived as unkind, she said, "I'm just about done, but perhaps you could lift that box of files over there onto the credenza?"

In the few minutes that he'd been in the room, Nikki felt a degree of fragility in Jim. Not physical, but more like someone who was mending from something. The two of them carried through the preparations for the day ahead, and Nikki could see that keeping Jim involved was helping put him at greater ease. "Are you ready for today?" she asked, trying to keep their conversation going.

Jim frowned, casting his eyes out the window to the cityscape below. "To be honest, I don't know what to expect. I've never been asked to be involved in something this important. As far as I know, my family has never done anything like this. They've never been big on our internal family communication. Is this going to end up being one big fight? My parents certainly don't need that. My sister Fanny can go off like a rocket …"

"I understand how you feel. You aren't the first family to feel that way, but what our other families have found is that Roger, Carrie and Tom provide a time-tested and proven support system for families like yours. You're all in good hands."

When they'd finished setting up, Jim took a seat at the round table, took out a rumpled notepad from his back pocket and started looking at what was written on it. The door chime rang and Nikki left the room to see who had arrived.

Roger popped his head in the door to say good morning and told Jim that the others were just arriving as well so they would be starting soon. Jim was soon joined by his mother, Al, Inge, Jeff and Jennifer. The group was complete when Fanny arrived, followed shortly by Dan. Tom and Carrie took a seat at the large table as well, after greeting each member of the Fortune family.

Roger, who would lead the session today, addressed any concerns that those who hadn't been in the other meetings might have had in his opening remarks. "As all of you know, our group has been working with Dan and Marnie for some months to assist in providing some clarity about their future options. Fanny, both you and Jeff have also been in for the meeting with the FCI people. We've met with everyone else at least once individually to hear your thoughts.

"Let me begin this day by making a request. We need your attention and we need your insight. We've asked you to prepare yourselves for today with a few simple questions in the agenda we sent you. You'll see behind me a model that I've drawn. We call it the F^3 system, and when it's completed by a family like yours it helps define the strengths and challenges an entrepreneur with a privately held company typically faces. The three perspectives it addresses are *Founder*, *Firm* and *Family*. You'll also note that each arm has a numerical scale and that two of the scales, *Founder* and *Firm*, have been filled in and the third, *Family*, has been left blank. Today's session will focus mainly on the *Family* arm and will complete an overall picture of where you sit as a family. By helping to identify the various strengths and weaknesses, we're able to determine what options are available for succession purposes.

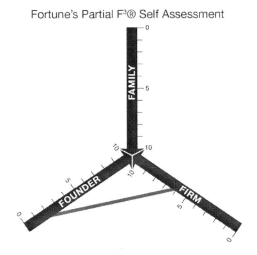

"Before we get started, I want to open the discussion to anyone who may have a question or comment." Marnie raised her hand. "Marnie?" he said.

"I want you all to remember what your Grandpa Farver always said whenever your aunts and I had a conversation that involved seeking out our varied viewpoints. 'None of us is as smart as all of us,'" she told her family. "Al, Jen, you're both part of this, too. Everyone is welcome to make a comment. Aren't they, Dan?" She gave his elbow a prod.

Dan got to his feet and looked around at his family. "Yes. It's important that we all feel comfortable to speak. We thought by taking this off site and away from any of our homes that we could encourage openness in all of us. I know I haven't been the best at this type of inclusiveness over the years, but better late than never.

"I want to tell you three stories. I think we all know enough about how I got started and the assistance I got from having an initial small investor who believed in me and then later Jennifer's father, my dear friend Ben, who got me involved in the Curtis Development Corporation. It all worked out far beyond our dreams," he said, looking at Marnie.

"During all this, FCI staffed up and we were blessed with people who wanted to work with us, supply us and allow us to grow." The room became still as Dan continued. "I know most of you know many of the people I'm talking about—RJ and others. But there are still many not known to all of you—or me, for that matter—who joined FCI and, over the years, it became how they made their way through life, too.

"When they or their kids needed money for clothing, shoes or medical expenses, when they wanted to buy a car or a house, save for their children's education or put those children in after-school activities and sports leagues, FCI was the engine to make that happen."

Dan swallowed before continuing, and Marnie knew he was fighting his emotions explaining what it all meant to him. "Then later, when they would take a vacation, put in a backyard pool, maybe buy a fishing boat or take care of parents who had grown old, FCI was there to provide that opportunity to earn. It was like a bank account where they could make withdrawals in exchange for their efforts. One of my own motivators was always that I didn't want to mess up that bank for them. Together, those families and our family forged a moral contract, and we all had a stake in the success of FCI. It was nice to see it all happen then and continue to happen now.

"I'm sure you all realize there were communities and neighborhoods that were built and customers came to depend on us to be there, ready to meet their requirements as they fed their children and raised their families. Those people allowed us to be who we became as a company and ..." He paused to look over his glasses at his family. "Who *we* became ...

"The last story I want to tell you, before you all make your own contribution to our discussion, is about all of you. In the midst of it you all came along, and it felt good to know that there would be a next generation. I know I left you all on your own, way too many times, as you grew up. I didn't attend a lot of recitals, school plays or games.

"If you could ask a hundred people like me, who've gained some measure of success, why they do what they do and why they work such long hard hours to do it, almost all of them would say it's so their families could have great lives. There's a paradox in that response, as pursuing this goal becomes all-encompassing and you start to live it as your existence. Your family is along for the ride whether they want to be or not. The very actions you take to achieve things take you from that family you claim to care about. There's a give and take, and it doesn't matter how much money you can accumulate, the clock has the same 24 hours for you as it does for everyone else.

"I want to say that I *do* care about all of you, what we built and my responsibilities that come with that. Finding that dividing line between the two was impossible for me. I realize that, but now is the time for me to start looking at my options," Dan said, finishing up his comments.

After a pause to see if anyone would respond, Roger used Dan's comments as an opening to draw out the family's individual points of view.

He had asked the group to respond to several of the same questions and scenarios as some of them had the day when the FCI people had met. They'd also been asked to branch out into their individual objectives, including those that revolved around their existing or potential involvement in FCI.

Jim went first, and told his family for the first time that he would rather be given the opportunity to be more independent of the resources of FCI. He wondered if there was a way to get the seed capital for his new business now, so he could operate on his own.

Dan had been aware of Jim's intention to strike out on his own, and while he didn't feel there was any scalability in the concept of vintage vehicles, he knew it made sense for Jim. His youngest was going to follow his own path and that path didn't include FCI. Besides, it might be fun to be involved as Jim's advisor. He had trouble with having to hive off a chunk of family capital to satisfy what was going to be required, though, especially considering Jim's recent history.

Dan led into what he was thinking with a question. "What's all this money for? I sat in this room several weeks ago with your mother, Roger and Carrie, and we had a long talk about that exact subject. Money is really about enabling more of life's options to be realized and it's what we need to think of here today, isn't it? All of you will need to pursue your own interests and passions. Find your own definition of success."

Jeff jumped into the conversation. ""Roger, if I recall correctly, I think that you worked through a similar issue in your work with the Curtis family. Shouldn't Jimmy be thinking of his own family, should that happen?"

Looking across the table, Jeff said, "Jimmy, I know that seems like a long way off, but you might run into the right person for you today. Life doesn't give you any warning. You might have children four or five years from now. Do you really want to gamble on your own plan when you can probably pursue what you want and still stay involved in FCI? I believe in you—I really do—but my sense tells me we may all regret it if we let you slip out of this."

Roger said, "Jeff is correct, and there might be a way to protect the interests of Jim's future family and any participation they might want in FCI down the road. Jim, you may wish to continue your participation in FCI as a shareholder, but for your own business aspirations, a loan could be structured with favorable terms and conditions to get you that starting capital."

Jim nodded, taking in this option, which he hadn't considered. He was adamant about getting out and being independent, but he was starting to enjoy being at the "big table" today and felt good about his inclusion in the discussion.

"I've noted this for follow up," Carrie said. "Now, Inge, how do you see your future?"

As Inge had told the team in her individual meeting, she liked the idea of staying on as a shareholder. Her immediate needs were met. She told her family that she didn't feel much need for the trappings of wealth for herself, but admitted that it would interest her to be a shareholder, and it would be a learning experience as well. In her charitable pursuits she'd been part of some volunteer boards like the art gallery and could see the value of learning the ropes of corporate governance that came out of a more traditional environment like FCI.

When asked whether she could stay out of the matters of the executive even if that managing shareholder was a family member, she paused and then said, "It depends. Jeff has been there all my life and I trust him. I know that Fanny has been an active participant in the company for a long time, but will she just go her own way or will she listen to a board of directors?"

Then, speaking forcefully for maximum impact, Inge added, "I will not be anyone's rubber stamp. If we take that route, whoever's in charge cannot count on me to support their decisions just because I'm family." Carrie noted that Inge had avoided looking at Fanny when she delivered her response.

Inge told the group that she also looked forward to involving her parents in the foundation and needed help in formalizing its board of directors.

257

"We'll talk, Inge," Dan said, smiling. "But that foundation has to start to reflect all of our family's interests."

"I guess I just have to help you understand what's important in the world, Dad," Inge replied.

Jeff and Jen gave their presentation as equals. Jen started first. She said that she had also experienced this process with her own family and that the model itself was ideal in giving equal status to Dan and Marnie's requirements, and FCI as the source of wealth, but also the family. It was a good way to tackle what she remembered as an otherwise daunting task.

"My mother and father wanted to create some type of legacy for everybody and they included CDC in their definition of *everybody*. I was younger than my siblings and maybe my perspective is closer to Inge's. I'm very fulfilled by the philanthropic management that my father has entrusted to me. I still am a shareholder in CDC and we've found that with my brother Kevin in charge it has worked.

"I've also heard of other situations where it didn't work, but I guess what we did was right for us. It was important to my father to make it all work, and he gave up certain things in the transition that were hard for him to do. He told me once that because my grandfather Curtis had done a lot of the initial land accumulation, he'd felt fortunate to be part of it and to have helped enlarge it. My father saw his role as one of guardianship of the family and our wealth throughout his entire working life. And now, he's come to realize that providing support for things like the medical program at UWI is his greater purpose.

"There's no good reason why our Fortune family can't do something similar," she said. She ended her comments there, but realized there were still obstacles in the room to getting to a good outcome that everyone could embrace.

Jeff now took over and said, "If what I'm being asked to do here is decide where we should all go with this, I'm not the person to ask. I want to run FCI. I won't make any bones about that."

Roger watched as a dark cloud seemed to pass over Fanny, but she said nothing.

"I've wanted to follow my father since I started there as a part timer in the stores," Jeff continued. "I think FCI needs to continue to innovate on its back end. My group is looking at packaging and, with some new equipment acquisitions, we can lower our costs in almost every department in the stores.

"Jen and I have talked about the future of our children as well. We want to expose them to everything we can. They will be global citizens. They have been to see their other grandfather and seen his clinic, and we're trying to raise them with his sense of humanitarian obligation. We want them to understand the fortunate position they've been born into. Jen and I are also fearful that too much money might limit their drive and independence.

"What we want is to nurture their capacity to demand more of themselves. If everything stayed static and our generation properly managed what we've been given, we wouldn't be responsible for a generation that doesn't get its own opportunity to win."

Al spoke up. "Can I say something about what I see here? I'm the only one in this room that truly came from nothing."

"Oh c'mon, Al. Don't give us that. How about Dad?" Inge responded.

"I realize that Dan came out of a pretty lean situation, too, but before his father died, it sounds like he didn't know it at the time, and that's a big difference to a child. I'm sure it hit him like a sledgehammer when he came back to help his mother out and discovered the mess that he, Uncle Peter and his mom were in.

"I'm not denying that his story is a terrific one. The reason it's terrific and one to retell is that those stories don't happen often. Any story we tell each other has a piece of fascination in it, doesn't it?"

Al started to speak with a softer tone as his memories took over and he led them down the path to what his own reality had been. "Dan and Marnie worked hard. It certainly helps, but hard work alone doesn't guarantee success. Growing up, I saw my parents work themselves to the bone, and some years it worked out alright, but there were others when we did exactly the same thing and it didn't," he explained as the others sat silent.

"I grew up in a different situation. As a child you can get a sense of impending doom—it's evident in your parents' faces. It feels like no matter what, your own destiny is to end up as the flotsam and jetsam of a storm you can't avoid.

"You all know that I came from the west—my parents were ranchers. We had cattle and tried to keep horses when we could feed them. I can remember some droughts as a boy that ended terribly for us. If feed crops didn't grow, we didn't have as much for the herd, and the horses were the first to go one way or another. We would build up our cattle herds only to have to sell them off after a drought or go broke trying to purchase feed for them to keep it all going. We walked a path between failure and hope every day. We were totally reliant on the weather and volatile commodity markets."

Tom, who had been as enthralled with Al's story as the rest, sensed that his comments to the Fortunes had moved the room's mindset to a more inclusive one in defining themselves.

"Whatever gets decided and when it gets decided, I'm going to support Dan and Marnie's wishes," Al continued. "They've led this family well for so many years and I don't think bickering between us in the second generation is proper. Let's keep our situation in perspective; trying to plan on how to handle all this money is a great problem to have."

Seeing an entry point into her husband's comments, Fanny corrected him. "We're actually the third generation, Al. Double F was long gone by the time I came along, but I knew my grandmother well, and we came to be in this business through them.

"I went to visit her by myself as a little girl on at least two occasions. My recollection is that she lived extremely modestly. She would apologize for things like her black-and-white TV. I just loved going there and the interest she took in me. She would bake and let me help. She had this popcorn maker that she would shake over the burner on her old gas range that made the greatest popcorn. I wish I could have spent more time there."

Marnie blanched, wondering if her eldest felt she hadn't spent enough time with her.

Roger had a sense from the others that they hadn't been expecting these reminiscences from Fanny. This softer side was coming from a place of vulnerability. In the one-to-one meetings, Fanny had come in with Al. They had discussed their own financial situation and disclosed that Fanny was the major breadwinner in their relationship. Al was content to be on the farm.

Fanny had asked Roger directly whether a sale of FCI was being considered and, if so, why. Roger had drawn her back from this line of thought and explained that her parents were considering their options and, in situations like these, selling always came up. He'd assured her they were at the start of the assessment process and no decision had been made.

She'd told the team that she considered herself the obvious choice to run FCI beyond her father's tenure. Like her father, she explained, she found a great deal of her own identity was tied to staying involved with things in the business. Fanny felt that, besides her father, she was easily the Fortune most identified with FCI and without that, she was at a loss to explain what to do next.

Financially, she and Al had put most of their money, her salary and her trust fund monies, into maintaining their lifestyle. They had always counted on some sort of major inheritance: higher salary, increased trust distributions, participation in dividends or a block of money to meet their ever increasing costs.

"I want you all to understand something about Al and me," Fanny had said. "You're all aware that Jen is a Curtis. She and Jeff have a lot more than the rest of us do. They could comfortably live on what she has alone. And Jeff pulls a nice salary out of FCI."

"We, on the other hand, do not have a second pot of money. I've thrown my life into FCI. We're not broke, but I feel vulnerable in two ways. We're not accumulating significant wealth outside FCI; we're living well and holding our heads above water. I believe my father would suffer in leaving FCI, but I have that same trait—it's my life, too." Fanny admitted to anticipating being totally lost without the social and political connections she'd made.

"I have great connections with the Department of Agriculture and the regulatory bodies," she'd said that day at GBA. "I live a very public life, being as politically active as I am. I can tell you there is a suggestion coming from others that I should consider a run for political office one day. That intrigues me.

"As I mentioned earlier, I'm concerned that, at least financially, Jeff doesn't have the real innate motivation to drive things forward beyond my father's departure."

Roger had reiterated that no decision had been made yet on whether to keep or sell the company. "If the decision was made to keep the company, could you foresee a point in time where you were 'in business' with your siblings?" Roger had asked Fanny.

Her response was that she'd anticipated that happening. If it did, she would like to keep Jeff involved, perhaps restructuring FCI's supply chain to become its own company with a tied relationship to FCI and crossover board appointments.

Roger volunteered an idea whereby Fanny would be the CEO and Jeff would be the COO. In the role of COO, Jeff could be tasked with maintaining an inward focus. Areas like supply chain distribution and overall quality control would be that role's purview.

The CEO would be externally directed and would lead current and future market strategy, customer satisfaction and other areas that would be defined through the board of directors. Finding balance between the roles would be the critical factor, but with a good governance structure, they could achieve that balance.

When he asked Fanny whether she thought they should keep the business/wealth together or did they want to go their separate ways, the businesswoman came out in her. "Of course, we should keep the business wealth together as a family. We are collectively stronger with a large investment pool." Fanny suggested that she would take the lead in getting others onside, but Al cautioned her that she couldn't come across as pushy.

Armed with this background information, Roger was not surprised the day of the family meeting to see a much more subdued Fanny. Whether it was out of financial or emotional dependence, Fanny had perhaps the most skin in the game of all of the family members. It wasn't clear whether her reticence was a strategic play or based upon her newly revealed vulnerability.

Without everyone understanding the background to her comments, the conciliatory tone of Fanny's message raised eyebrows around the table.

"I feel sick about losing Dan's guidance in FCI. It would be a real loss. I can't bear the thought of things changing from the way they are now. However, talking through all these old stories today and when we had the group from the company in has made me realize that we have to be prepared. We owe ourselves that.

"I realize I've done some things that might suggest I'm not the person to succeed, but I assure you all that I am motivated. We must do the right thing for FCI. You heard my father this morning and his ideas of the moral contract he feels so strongly about. I don't think I could be quite as poetic about it as he was, but I was floored by what he said. We owe our customers a lot, and it rang so true with me. Jeff is such a big part of this business, too, and I know I haven't always seemed appreciative of the role he has played, but we couldn't do it without him."

Roger finally broke the silence following Fanny's candid remarks. "Whether Dan's decision is to keep the business in the family or sell it and keep the proceeds together, there will be a number of diverse roles for you all to play as siblings, employees, owners and directors. In each of these roles, there are different questions to be addressed and forums in which to address them. Marnie has given us clear marching orders that whatever transpires, you are all still to be able to enjoy getting together with this family without an underlying business tension in the air." Marnie smiled.

"Whatever is decided, "continued Roger, "Dan has given us what we anticipate is sufficient lead time to be able to coach you through the roles you might be taking on. What we were looking for was a receptiveness to the guidance we can offer.

"I would like to draw you back to the last of the components of the F^3 model: the *Family*. I would like you all to spend a few moments, in light of the conversations today, to consider how much connectivity you feel with each other as a family and how this might impact on the ability of the group to grow into the new roles we've discussed."

Finding Clarity

Dan and Marnie lingered at the round table having a quiet discussion, after the rest of the family had left. After a half an hour, it appeared that their conversation was complete and Roger, Carrie and Tom filed back in to the meeting room.

The Fortunes' faces betrayed minds filled with mixed thoughts. Roger was a calming influence. "You may feel that your family giving themselves a score of 3 on the *Family* arm of the F^3 model is somehow bad. I can tell you, though, that the benefit of having used the model is to give clarity on where you stand and, depending on what ultimate outcome you and your family choose, we can certainly help you plan how to get there. The model has helped define our starting point.

"The good news on the family is that they're all coachable. No one was adamantly opposed to being part of the process in a way that's appropriate for their individual purposes. They demonstrated an openness to work together in the multiple roles they may be asked to fulfill as owners, employees, directors and family depending on what you'd like to do."

"I just want as much harmony in our family as we can have," Marnie reminded the others. "With all the resources available to us, it would be ridiculous if our children couldn't each have the opportunity to experience success in the way that works for them. The best inheritance I can imagine is for them to have the same sense of satisfaction for themselves as Dan has derived from FCI. I'm not sure that Fanny's siblings have completely bought in to her change of heart. I think we're in for a few rough moments, no matter what path Dan chooses."

Fortune's Impasse

"Our conclusion at this point is that the two of you have choices and perhaps more options than you think," said Carrie. "We didn't see anything that was that surprising. Nothing we've seen would place limits on your options. This process has also set the groundwork for open communication in the correct forum to deal with issues as they come up. Regardless of which path Dan chooses, everyone seems open to learning the new skills they will need as their roles take shape. We'll also help keep the pipes unclogged by developing their communication skills."

Roger explained, "What we will do now is brief you both on your options and where we can go from here."

"First, in looking at the model up here on the board, you can see that the *Founder* arm is a 2, the *Firm*'s a 6 and the *Family* is at 3." Roger drew a line connecting the three data points, plotted against the F^3 model. "Reflecting on what we've gleaned from all the meetings, I can tell you that, in succession terms, we're at the end of the beginning. You are well positioned to move forward from here."

Roger explained to Dan that the model revealed three main areas that needed some work:

- Dan's emotional dependency on the business and the reciprocal dependency or shadow he cast over FCI just by being who he was, in the marketplace and the industry.
- The selection of a new successor or successors and the readiness of the management team to work independently of Dan and with his successor or successors.
- The family's ability to grow into its new multiple roles.

Carrie told them, "We will take the model we have today and update it throughout the process. The idea is to work on the items we perceive are giving you the lower scores and get as close as we can to that tighter, smaller triangle we showed you before. As we improve in these areas, the likelihood of success—whatever path you chose—is increased."

The Fortunes asked if the F^3 model could be used to illustrate the updating of the next generation's individual plans from time to time. They particularly liked the model as a tool for the needs and expectations brought forward through the family meetings and the board of directors to help guide FCI strategic planning and capital deployment decisions.

Tom noted that, as a common methodology, F^3 would be an invaluable tool to help achieve alignment between the family strategic planning process and the FCI strategic planning process.

Roger concluded the day with a final thought. "In the end, your destiny is in your own hands. Take the time you need to consider what you've seen and heard. You have a getaway, I think. Go use it. Take yourselves out of your regular routine and the option that's right will come to you."

In the elevator on the way down to the parking lot, Dan said to Marnie, "I know where I'm going. Are you coming?"

Copper Beech

Dan arrived at the lake earlier than he'd expected. After the events of the last few days, he'd told Marnie he needed to decompress a bit. At most times of year he would fly up, but there'd been a storm front coming in. Dan prided himself on being a very safe pilot, but having had an in-flight scare a few years back, he was conscious of the elements that Mother Nature could throw at aviators who thought they had it all figured out. He would drive up this time.

The night before they were to depart, Marnie had surprised him by saying she'd be staying behind. "Danny, I don't think I'm going to come," Marnie told him when he arrived home from work.

Passing through the family room, he stopped and sat down on the arm of his wife's chair to listen to her. "This has been a demanding process for both of us. I'm tired, but really happy. We know where everyone stands and what the bigger picture looks like, thanks to the perspective we now have," Marnie told him.

"I think you need to take stock of what all this means to you and get your distance from it for as long as it takes you to commit in your own mind. They showed us some very sound processes for making this work, but you are the trigger on this and you need to be sure," she said gently.

The next day, Dan set off. The plane was always the fastest and most fun, but there wasn't much traffic and he enjoyed the drive. He thought about what Marnie had said and the work that lay ahead as he pulled down the fire road that led to the cottage. Bringing the vehicle to a stop beneath the majestic canopy of his favorite landmark, the copper beech, Dan was going to unpack, but sat for a few minutes in the car with the ignition off as he thought about the decisions that would now be his alone to make.

What he'd learned about his life, his business and his future in the last several months was similar to the insights he'd gained from flying. The danger in each was in not having an accurate picture of where you were, at a given moment. More information was better than less.

He and Tom had discussed this at their lunch and found that they agreed on an important concept, that we develop skills through repetition. This was true whether it was about running the business, playing golf or even raising a family, but the moment you thought things were easy was the moment in which you were potentially exposed.

He now felt confident that there was a way to avoid the dangers that came with his position and with thinking about where to take things at this stage. Between Roger, Carrie and Tom, each arm of the F^3 model would be addressed in a personalized way. Having his family members engaged and the support of key people at FCI, Dan realized it wouldn't be easy, but they were light years ahead of where they could have been.

He jumped out of the car and unloaded his things. The daylight faded fast at this time of year and he wanted to get inside and make himself dinner.

The next day he did a few errands in the local village. The fellow at the gas station told him there might be a bit of bad weather and, noting the darkening skies, Dan headed back to the cottage. He thought he'd read a bit and take it easy.

After a few hours, he put his book aside, his mind eventually drifting back to the issue at hand. He picked up a pad of paper off Marnie's desk. Subconsciously he started to draw out the final version of the model that he, Marnie, the family and those from his firm had shaped. He made notes to himself about the factors driving the various scores and what would be needed to make advances in each area. The results made sense, he thought, and gave him the emotional distance from himself to properly support his ultimate decision.

Through the application of the model, he could see what had to be done in each of the following areas for a successful transition for his family:

- His own emotional ties to FCI and the firm's reliance on him
- The readiness of the FCI management team
- His family itself, creating future opportunity and fairness in how each was handled

Dan pulled away from looking over the F^3 diagram they had co-created and gazed out to the lake, as was his habit. It had always served to settle him, somehow, with the water lapping the shoreline.

The day had changed for the worse. Even seeing the shoreline through the gloom was a challenge, and much larger swells with whitecaps were forming as far as he could see. Looking out at the heavy clouds, it was clearly turning into a day made for introspection, as there wasn't going to be anything to draw his attention to the outdoors.

The weather was potent. Strong winds started to howl and rain began to team down. It rattled off the windowsill close to where he was working.

Dan moved into the kitchen and shut the windows. As he filled the kettle to make himself a cup of tea, his mind drifted back to his parents and to his father's ownership of the Market. The debt pressure on Double F had probably been terrible. As he had aged, Dan had intuitively come to realize that his father's death had been no accident. More likely, the pressure had probably caused his early demise.

His mother had gamely withstood the strife his father had caused, and he resolved that whatever happened through his own transition planning process, he wouldn't put Marnie through that. "Getting rich and not enjoying life" was a stupid outcome, as Ben had observed more than once in the last few months. And the message had started to hit home.

Thoughts of Ben were quickly followed by his memory of meeting Marnie at school on that day long ago. Knowing what he had learned over the years as a hobbyist with the mechanical toys in his life, he had eventually come to the conclusion that the failure of his car to start that day hadn't been a total fluke. That ignition wire had some help getting disconnected, and he was grateful that Marnie had tricked him.

The kettle was just starting to boil, and his memories pushed him further back into the early years of FCI, back to those that had been part of the story that followed. His mother, Mr. and Mrs. Davis, their daughter Ginny Curtis, Pudge, RJ, Beth and Bob, and those staff who had come and gone from FCI through the years. His mind created pictures of each, as well as images of many of those early regular customers, their names long forgotten, but not his appreciation of their loyalty. With a shiver, a flash of realization came over Dan; many of these people were no longer alive. He'd been a young man—a kid, really. Those days were some of the most exciting and satisfying times of his life.

Of course it hadn't started out that way. He hadn't thought of the first month or two as terribly exciting. In fact at that point, he'd thought his working life would always be like the banal and mundane early days at the original Market.

He eventually experienced those occasional emotional wins that allow entrepreneurs to persevere—figuring out how to get a display to look right, negotiating better sourcing with suppliers and watching his daily revenues slowly and gradually start to rise.

After that came his early days with Ben Curtis and the growth years; they were heady times, the fun of it all easier to pull from his memories than the challenges.

Throughout it all he had come to understand that exhilaration and despair were two sides of the same coin. Being in the trenches in the first place was the first requirement of success. There was no great win without that commitment. If you ran your own company, it was impossible to escape without wounds to mind, body and soul. Was everyone else ready to man that trench without him?

Am I being selfish, he asked himself. Were there people at FCI who could anticipate a different future for themselves? A future that would allow them to flourish in an FCI that evolved into something else if he stepped aside? Am I denying members of my family the elation that I found in it all? Were Fanny and/or Jeff able to take it from here?

As an entrepreneur who had won more than he'd lost, Dan had always reminded himself that there were always potential losses lurking. He fought the images that crowded his mind, images of all the possible future scenarios.

At that exact moment, an enormous bolt of lightning hit very close to the cottage. The structure reverberated as the air pocket collapsed in a rolling roar across the lakefront. In sequence, Dan could make out the hew and groan that could only have come from splitting and cracking timber. The resounding thud that followed shook the building to its foundations.

All electricity to the cottage and outbuildings had been knocked out. Grabbing a flashlight, he pulled on his raingear and headed out into the howling storm. His head bent, the brim of his hat acted as mere optimism in keeping the windswept sheets of rainfall from his eyes.

He cast his searchlight across the waterfront and gardens of his property. In the high wind he could hear the plaintive, weak wail of an alarm.

Approaching the corner, he suddenly knew what he would see. The top branches of a major tree lay across the entire driveway. Underneath, his vehicle had been hit squarely in the descent and the car horn weakly bleating its final notes soon gave up. The front half of the car was now less than twenty inches off the ground, having taken the direct impact of a heavy limb.

Everyone in the Fortune family had closely identified with the copper beech tree, and it was a loss. The children and grandchildren had climbed and

Fortune's Impasse

played on the rope swing Marnie had concocted from an old tractor tire years ago. The light in his hand illuminating the carnage eventually found the old tire, now lying useless amongst the wreckage.

Behind the car, Dan could see the trunk still stood. One of the downed limbs, Dan noted, had a girth of at least 30 inches where it had detached close to the trunk. Attempting to shield his eyes from the driving rain, he shone his light up into the darkness. He could tell that the copper had sustained a major, perhaps mortal, wound. It was now a dramatically scarred version of its former self. The previous owner of the Fortune compound had told him at purchase that it was over a hundred years old at that time.

Dan had always considered the copper eternal. He had thought of it with significant pride—symbolic in its strength and resiliency. He swallowed hard, taking a moment to come to grips with what it was now, knowing that no amount of money could restore it to its former glory. Nature and age didn't work like that.

He would take a further look in the morning, but in the meantime, nothing could be done. With a heavy heart, he headed back into the cottage.

The unsettled weather gradually left the lake. Later, alone in bed, he struggled to find sleep. He could see now that this decision, like all his past entrepreneurial decisions, would be played out as light and darkness.

For Dan, the darkness was an emotional shadow that cast itself over events and people. It signified indecision and fear—a debilitating lack of forward progress.

In light, he saw personal happiness, clarity, fairness, family affinity and in the end, love—love for himself, his wife, their family, his company and for those who had been a part of what FCI had become under his stewardship.

In the end, he decided all the transition complexity would distill down to a future where he had made a choice. Either he could cast his shadow, even from the grave, over the next Fortune generations and FCI as a negative invisible presence or he could leave his light.

Leaving his light would mean providing his insight and experiences to the others but not at the cost of denying them the critical element of trial and error, which was something every generation had to embrace as its own.

His and Marnie's own transition plan wouldn't be completed for some time yet. The model told him what needed to be addressed, though. He could see a way forward now to create the strength in others who would eventually outlive him. He realized that what he would do wasn't likely the path that others in his particular circumstance might take, but that each founder, family and firm was unique. Giving equal status to and honoring each element was the right thing to do for anyone with a privately held company.

His own commitment and resolution to his future path—to this light—occurred before his eyes closed and he drifted off into a restful sleep.

The early light of the day eventually crept in the window and found Dan in that midpoint between being asleep and awake. He hadn't felt this at peace with himself in a very long time, and he'd enjoyed a restful night. The agreement he'd made with himself the previous evening had stood the unconscious test of sleeping on it.

He opened the window blinds to the kind of day that lakefront properties were invented for. He saw the massive copper beech and, where the colossal main limb had eventually come to rest—his car lying beneath it—it was quite clear he wouldn't be driving it home.

From this vantage point, he studied the tree some more. The large limb that had come down was one of three of equal stature and dimension. The copper would need to be checked out by an arborist for unseen damage and safety, of course, but in the light of day, it was still a thing of beauty. Damaged, yes, but mortally? He hoped not.

While it would never be the tree it had been just the day before, it would still leave a certain impression on all who experienced its newly evolved shape.

"Kind of like me," he said aloud as he closed his bedroom door and padded barefoot down the hall to start the new day.

Postscript

Note to the readers of Fortune's Impasse:

You may wonder why our story ends at this point. Why didn't we pursue it to its ultimate resolution?

Most of our readers have their own legacy to consider and each would be unique to the individuals, family and firms involved. The purpose of this book is to introduce to the reader, and help the reader understand, a solution process, in this case, F^3.

We have found that the model takes into account the multidimensional perspectives relevant to many as they carry out their own analysis of their family legacy. The greater purpose of this book is to paint a picture of a family, the Fortunes, that struggle with the issue of clarity in pursuit of a good outcome for themselves, their firm and ultimately their fortune.

We all strive to live lives with purpose and success, as Dan and Marnie have in this fictional case. In all families, ups and downs occur. Just as positive events and breaks can happen, so, too, can unforeseen circumstances brought on by business setbacks, health issues, family breakdown, or personal investment loss. Succession is a process that needs more time, a "longer runway," than most families give it. And time is the enemy.

The value in reading this book is to get to the crux of where succession planning goes awry, and to get to this earlier rather than later, when options become more limited.

Thank you and please touch base with us at Fortunesimpasse.com for blog articles and access to the community of readers who are pursuing solutions in this critical area of family wealth management.

About the Authors

Tim Maloney has been tied closely to his own entrepreneurial ventures for over two decades, while also providing guidance to over 1500 businesses ranging from start-ups to those that are large, well established and multi-generational. His clients often come from family-owned privately held companies that are trying to close the gap between their strategy and execution. He describes his past, present and future client relationships as evolving, ongoing, limitless conversations to encourage and secure effectiveness within these enterprizes and their shareholder families.

You can reach Mr. Maloney at tmaloney@newportgroup.ca or at Tim@fortunesimpasse.com

Fortune's Impasse

Randy McLachlan has advised families and their businesses from traditional professional practices, including accounting firms, law firms, a registered brokerage firm, a major Canadian bank and its investment counseling firm and an independently-owned investment counseling firm. Randy co-founded Genbridge, a family office, in order to better integrate these disciplines and serve individuals, families and their businesses. Throughout his various professional experiences, one repetitive theme emerged – that of families looking to successfully transition their wealth, including their businesses. The Genbridge multidisciplinary platform provides families with the unique opportunity to analyze the succession options available to them from a central point of contact while incorporating the perspectives of the founders, firm and family, while giving due consideration to both the "people" and "technical" issues which come into play.

You can reach Randy at rmclachlan@genbridge.ca or at randy@fortunesimpasse.com.